Regeneration and Renewal

Also published by Canterbury Press

The Parish: People, Place and Ministry – A Theological and Practical Exploration
Editor Malcolm Torry

'a timely, stimulating and, above all, encouraging account of parish ministry by practitioners who clearly believe in it, enjoy it and are good at it ... warmly recommended'. *Church Times*

Diverse Gifts: Varieties of Lay and Ordained Ministry in the Church and Community
Editor Malcolm Torry

'a treasure trove of pastoral insights ... those involved in, or training for, any kind of ministry should find it useful'. *CR Quarterly*

Ordained Local Ministry: A New Shape for Ministry in the Church of England
Editors Malcolm Torry and Jeffrey Heskins

A landmark volume and the first in-depth study of this contemporary model of priesthood.

www.canterburypress.co.uk

Regeneration and Renewal

The Church in New and Changing Communities

Edited by
Malcolm Torry

CANTERBURY
PRESS

Norwich

© The contributors 2007

First published in 2007 by the Canterbury Press Norwich
(a publishing imprint of Hymns Ancient & Modern
Limited, a registered charity)
9–17 St Alban's Place, London N1 0NX

www.scm-canterburypress.co.uk

British Library Cataloguing in Publication data

A catalogue record for this book is available
from the British Library

ISBN 978-1-85311-800-5

Typeset by Regent Typesetting, London
Printed and bound in Great Britain by
William Clowes Ltd, Beccles, Suffolk

Contents

Acknowledgements   vii

Foreword   ix

About the Contributors   xi

1 Regeneration and Renewal: New and Changing
   Communities and the Church   1
   MALCOLM TORRY

2 Regeneration in Southwark: A Political View   9
   JEREMY FRASER

3 Knowing the Facts: The Church's Collection of the
   Information it Needs   19
   CATRIONA ROBERTSON

4 Thinking Long-term: Keeping Going at the
   Elephant and Castle   36
   NEIL MCKINNON

5 In the Middle of It: Co-operation and Resistance
   on the Ferrier Estate   49
   NICK RUSSELL AND CHARLIE INGRAM

6 Now It's Done: The North Peckham Estate after
   the Makeover   62
   JIM JELLEY

7 Up It Goes: The Church among North Southwark's
   New Financial District   73
   TIM SCOTT

8   Creating Space: The Aylesbury Estate and the
    InSpire Project   83
    GILES GODDARD

9   Redeeming Sacred Space: St John's, Angell Town   93
    MARTIN CLARK

10 Renewing the Culture: The Church on the
    South Bank   104
    RICHARD TRUSS

11 Starting from Scratch: The Greenwich Peninsula   114
    MALCOLM TORRY

12 Congregations Are Mission: Building
    Congregations in Thamesmead   131
    JEDIDAH ENOCH-ONCHERE AND
    SIMON BOXALL

13 Lots To Do: Project Development   143
    SUE HUTSON

14 Thinking Wider: Coping with the Thames
    Gateway   155
    MALCOLM TORRY

Conclusion: Building God's City   168
    MALCOLM TORRY

Glossary   173

Acknowledgements

I am grateful to all those people who have contributed to this book: to Canon Graham Shaw and the Revd Tim Scott for help with planning it; to the authors, and to all those who have been willing to talk to us or correspond with us as we have prepared our chapters; to those who have commented on our drafts; to the Revd Andrew Davey for help with literature for Chapter 1 and for the concluding chapter; to the Bishop of Woolwich, the Rt Revd Christopher Chessun, for his Foreword and his support for those of us working in parishes containing regeneration projects; and particularly to Christine Smith of the Canterbury Press for her enthusiasm for this project.

I am also grateful to all those who have contributed to my own involvement in issues related to urban regeneration and renewal: to the patrons of the Parish of East Greenwich and to Bishop Peter Hall for appointing me to be team rector of the parish containing the Greenwich Peninsula; and to the parish, to the chaplaincy team at the Millennium Dome during 2000, and to all those involved in the current development of the Greenwich Peninsula: colleagues at Meridian Delta Ltd, Sir Robert McAlpine, and Anschutz Entertainment Group, and the trustees, chaplains and Council of Reference of the Greenwich Peninsula Chaplaincy. A particularly useful gathering is that of archdeacons and others who relate to the Thames Gateway in their dioceses, and I would like to thank its convenor, the Venerable Christine Hardman, Archdeacon of Lewisham, for involving me in her responsibility for the Thames Gateway in the Diocese of Southwark and for her active support for the Greenwich Peninsula Chaplaincy.

Foreword

The Church is in the business of regeneration and renewal. Nowhere is this felt more keenly than in the 'world in a city' which is London, where the global so rapidly becomes the local and concepts like tolerance come to life in the practice of hospitality and the forging of friendships. In new and changing urban communities, into which capital resources continue to pour, it takes courage to tackle the scandal presented by continuing pockets of deprivation, despair and isolation. Poverty remains the reality of urban living for many and cannot be ignored amid so much wealth and prosperity.

The editor and contributors to this book are to be congratulated for placing theological reflection firmly in the context of their presence and engagement as practitioners in South London. With telling insights and zeal for the gospel, they describe the opportunities for renewing communities spiritually around major regeneration initiatives that can all too easily become developer-led unless there are critical partnerships and an equal concern for building spiritual capital. Caring for souls as well as forming 'a critical rather than a docile partnership with the agencies of regeneration and development'[1] is a sign of the Church's enduring commitment to local communities over long periods of time, working willingly with people of different or no faith for the common good.

We learn about the impact on people's lives of rapid change and vibrant interactions: but we must read on! Regeneration of old estates demands strategies for community renewal that are life-enhancing and address fragmentation. The commercial capital that will transform north Southwark needs to embrace rather than expel the resident population, starting with programmes to help people to improve their skills. Where people begin to believe in themselves, in life as sacred and individuals as connected, there is hope and space for everyone to flourish. The confluence of the many new communities evolving in the Thames Gateway and the new developments that will be left behind by the Olympic Games is already linking what is described in these chapters with the next ten years, flowing out beyond Deptford, the Greenwich Peninsula, Woolwich Arsenal and Thamesmead, with enormous consequences for the river-bound urban landscape and the lives of vast numbers of people in our great world city and nation.

It is a fascinating narrative that I commend to you warmly.

The Rt Revd Christopher Chessun
Bishop of Woolwich

Note

1 Commission on Urban Life and Faith, *Faithful Cities: A Call for Celebration, Vision and Justice*, Church House Publishing/Methodist Publishing House, London, 2006, § 1.24.

About the Contributors

Simon Boxall was ordained in the Norwich Diocese in 1979 where he served his curacy. In 1984 he left for Brazil with the South America Mission Society. Initially he worked in a highly industrial setting in the city of Belo Horizonte, but after that he worked mainly in small rural towns until he moved to Rio de Janeiro where he was the chaplain to the English-speaking people of that city and area. He left there in January 2005 to take up his present post as a team vicar in Thamesmead.

Martin Clark has been vicar of three parishes in the Diocese of Southwark since 1977. Since 1998 he has been vicar of St John the Evangelist, Angell Town in Brixton, in the London Borough of Lambeth.

Jedidah Enoch-Onchere is the managing director of Deans London and North London ITeC. Her work focuses on regeneration programmes. After her PhD in Soil Chemistry from Reading University, Jedidah embarked on a career of setting up new organizations and training centres in the Voluntary Sector and also as a UN consultant for the environment. She has held various lay positions in the Church of England.

Jeremy Fraser trained at London Bible College (1977–9) and awaited God's call. When he could not hear any particular call, he became a postman and then a social worker. He joined the Labour Party at a time when most people were leaving, and became a councillor and then leader of Southwark Council. In 1997 he was a parliamentary candidate against fellow Christian Simon Hughes. He is married to Ruth and has two teenagers (Jake and Isla) and they all live in Peckham. He is in the second year of his ordination training with the South Eastern Institute for Theological Education.

Giles Goddard is rector of St Peter's, Walworth, and area dean of Southwark and Newington. Before ordination, he was director of the Southwark and London Diocesan Housing Association and involved in regeneration schemes across London.

Sue Hutson has an MA in community development and has been involved in community development for the past six years. She has a breadth of experience, working at grassroots, parish and diocesan levels. She is keen to see that local communities are heard and respected, and individuals empowered to make a difference to their own lives and their community's life in ways that are honest, just, and sustainable. Her role in the Diocese of Southwark is to work with parish churches, especially those in areas of multiple deprivation, to establish projects that serve the local community. Sue also teaches on various schemes and is a trustee of a community development charity in Kent.

Charlie Ingram is a Baptist minister working on the Ferrier Estate in Kidbrooke, south-east London. He is minister of Holy Spirit Church which works in partnership with other local Christians in mission on the estate. Under the banner of Ferrier Focus, Anglicans, Baptists, free Evangelicals and a local Christian charity are working together to show God's love on the estate. He has also worked in marketing and as a musician. He is married to Sarah and has three children.

Jim Jelley was a probation officer before being ordained as a priest in the Church of England in 1981. He has spent his ministry in parishes in South London in the Diocese of Southwark and has been vicar of St Luke's, Peckham, for ten years. He loves music and cricket and continues to sing and play.

Neil McKinnon was born and raised in London north of the Thames. He crossed the river to be ordained in Southwark Cathedral in 1974. Since then he has worked in Deptford, the St Helier Estate, Lambeth, and the Thamesmead Christian Community, and he is now the rector of St Matthew's at the Elephant and Castle.

Catriona Robertson is a fan of the theologian Howard Thurman, who wrote, 'Do not ask what the world needs: ask what brings you alive and do that, because what the world needs is people who are alive.' A psychology graduate, Catriona worked in community projects in London, Calcutta and Papua New Guinea before becoming closely involved with an innovative parish church community in South London. She is committed to inter-faith and peace-building work and lives in South London with her husband and two teenage children.

Nick Russell read modern languages at Cambridge and went to work at GCHQ. He became involved in part-time church youth and community work on a deprived estate. He joined Church Army in 1996 and was offered the post on the Ferrier Estate in 1999.

Tim Scott read theology at Exeter University, then worked with homeless people in the King's Cross area of London. He trained for the priesthood at Westcott House, Cambridge, and was ordained in 1987. After serving a curacy in Romford he spent five years as a community priest in Walthamstow on two housing estates undergoing major regeneration. He spent a further seven years as a parish priest in Leytonstone, working closely with the local authority and a housing action trust. Following two years working on clergy training issues, he was appointed in 2004 as rector of Christ Church, Blackfriars, and the Bishop of Southwark's Regeneration Adviser.

Malcolm Torry is team rector in the East Greenwich team ministry, vicar of St George's Westcombe Park, chaplain to the Tate and Lyle refinery on Greenwich Peninsula, and site chaplain to the new development on the peninsula. Before ordination, he worked for the Department of Health and Social Security. Following ordination, he was curate at St Matthew's, Newington, at the Elephant and Castle, then curate at Christ Church, Southwark, and industrial chaplain with the South London Industrial Mission, and then vicar of St Catherine's, Hatcham, at New Cross. He is married with three children.

Richard Truss is vicar of St John with St Andrew, Waterloo. He has spent most of his ministry in London parishes both north and south of the river. He is senior chaplain of the Actors Church Union, and chaplain to the Royal National Theatre, the Young Vic, and the South Bank Centre. He is an honorary canon of Southwark Cathedral.

1. Regeneration and Renewal

New and Changing Communities and the Church

MALCOLM TORRY

Then I saw a new heaven and a new earth; for the first heaven and the first earth had passed away, and the sea was no more. And I saw the holy city, the new Jerusalem, coming down out of heaven from God, prepared as a bride adorned for her husband. And I heard a loud voice from the throne saying,
'See, the home of God is among mortals.
He will dwell with them;
they will be his peoples,
and God himself will be with them;
he will wipe every tear from their eyes.
Death will be no more;
mourning and crying and pain will be no more,
for the first things have passed away.'
And the one who was seated on the throne said, 'See, I am making all things new.' (Revelation 21.1–5)

This is a book of stories about South London's communities and churches (mainly its Church of England parishes). Each story is about a changing place, a changing community, and a changing Church. Each story is about 'regeneration':

Regenerate: 1. regrow (new tissue); 2. bring new and more vigorous life to (an area or institution); 3. (especially in Christian use) give a new and higher spiritual nature to (*Compact Oxford English Dictionary*).[1]

It's clearly the second definition of 'regenerate' that we're mainly talking about here, for the stories are about bringing new and more vigorous life to places and communities, about bringing new and more vigorous life to the Church, and about how a changing Church and a changing community affect each other.

But not everything that is called 'regeneration' results in 'renewal' – that is, new and more vigorous life – or, rather, it may result in more vigorous life for some but not for others. This is an issue that you, the reader, might like to keep in mind as you read. You will find yourself asking more questions: 'How can the Church contribute to the regeneration process so that it results in new and more vigorous life for everyone in a community, and especially the poorest?' 'How can new and changing communities contribute to new and more vigorous life in our churches?' 'What are the connections between the second and third definitions of "regenerate"?'

And what constitutes 'regeneration'? (The definitions above don't answer this question.) The definitions tell us what the results are, but not what it *is*. So the question for us is this: 'What does "regeneration" mean when it's used to refer to what's going on along the south bank of the Thames from Deptford to Thamesmead, or in Angell Town, or on the Ferrier Estate in Kidbrooke?' Does it, as Robert Furbey suggests, mean something really rather conservative? Does it imply state decision-making and the further marginalization of the already marginal? [2] Or does it mean a process that involves the whole of the community in seeking a renewed built environment and a renewed community with the well-being and integration of all of its diverse members as its main aim? Certain government, local authority and church circles use the term 'regeneration' all the time: and because it's used so often, those who use it don't offer definitions. It's a bit like Jesus' parables concerning the kingdom of God. He tells us about the kingdom, but he doesn't define it. He doesn't need to. And so with 'regeneration'. It's as we discuss it that we learn what we're talking about, and we learn how broad a concept it can be: it's about buildings; about education and healthcare provision; about safety in our homes and on the streets; about fulfilling work; about sufficient money to live on; about participation in decision-making; about knowing the people among whom we live; about diversity and the acceptance and valuing of diversity. Such a list could be a very long one.

> It's about building *capital*: the built environment, the transport infrastructure, community, educational and healthcare facilities, . . . Capital Formation: personal, physical, financial, intellectual, social, human, . . . [3]

But as this book will show, 'regeneration' is even broader than that, because it's also about the building of *spiritual* capital, and about

ways in which spiritual and other kinds of capital interact with one
another.

This process has been on the Church's agenda since Jesus told his
parables, because the kingdom of God he lived and spoke about is
the community of justice and peace of our God-given hope.

But the agenda was sharpened in 1985 when the Archbishop's
Commission on Urban Priority Areas published the report *Faith in
the City* which made recommendations to both nation and Church:
recommendations intended to result in 'regeneration' (p. 171). The
recent *Faithful Cities* celebrates the 'faithful capital' that the
Commission on Urban Life and Faith has found around our cities,
and makes recommendations, again both to nation and Church, for
the sustaining of 'faithful capital', or, as I have called it, 'spiritual
capital'.

Just how diverse this spiritual capital is, and just how diverse are
the contexts in which it exercises its influence and from which it
receives its inspiration, should become clear as you read.

Following this first chapter that asks questions about the whole
notion of 'regeneration', Jeremy Fraser describes the regeneration of
a large part of the London Borough of Southwark from the view-
point of a local politician, and Catriona Robertson shows us how to
gather facts about our communities (a necessary preliminary to any
participation in regeneration and renewal).

Then come chapters about the Church's relationship to regeneration projects in particular areas: Neil McKinnon on long-term
involvement at the Elephant and Castle; Nick Russell and Charlie
Ingram on their very different roles in relation to the regeneration of
the Ferrier Estate in the London Borough of Greenwich; Jim Jelley
on a church's relationship with a project nearing completion in
Southwark; and Tim Scott on a congregation's relationship to high-
rise office development in North Southwark.

Then follow two chapters offering different perspectives on the
relationship between church buildings to regeneration and renewal.
Giles Goddard shows how regeneration and renewal in a community can result in the regeneration of a church building, and
Martin Clark narrates how the regeneration of a church building has
contributed to the renewal of a local community.

Richard Truss tells us about the Church's contribution to the
renewal of culture: an important ingredient in any community
renewal, but particularly important on the South Bank. The editor
tells the story of the Church's relationship with a completely new
community on the Greenwich Peninsula; and Jedidah Enoch-
Onchere and Simon Boxall describe the Church's involvement with
the renewal of an existing community in central Thamesmead and

its engagement with a completely new community in West Thamesmead. Sue Hutson's chapter offers valuable experience in project development; the editor takes a bus ride from Deptford to Thamesmead; and we conclude with reflections on signposts towards the City of God.

The regeneration process is incorrigibly diverse, and intertwined in it are places, communities and individuals. It really is not possible to deal with them separately, and this book does not attempt to do so; but by the time you get to our conclusions you will have discovered changed communities, changed individuals, changed places, and changed churches. The influence is always multi-directional, with congregations and their activities being changed by the regeneration of places and communities at least as much as they contribute to the wider regeneration process. The regeneration of communities can regenerate churches – but I say 'can' advisedly, for it is equally possible for rapid regeneration to send congregations into their shells, frightened by the rapid change around them. In such situations the wider Church must support threatened congregations and see the problem as a symptom of a regeneration that might not be regeneration at all. If the changing of places doesn't result in new freedom, hope and opportunity for communities and the people who belong to them, then sharp prophecy might be required of the Church. There are examples of such prophetic activity in some of the chapters of this book. But where it's working as it should, the Church and other faith communities can be important community-builders in new and changing communities, and can themselves be significantly enriched by changes going on around them.

Faith in the City had things to say about relationships between different faith communities. It is a sign of the times that the new *Faithful Cities* takes the faith communities working together as axiomatic and regards the Church as one faith community among others. This is today's experience, and this has been our experience. In a world in which people move more easily from one country to another, communication gets ever broader and faster, and peace between different religions is going to be essential for our survival, it will be essential for the faith communities to work together. One of the questions that you might find yourself pondering as you finish the book will be a question about the extent to which the different faiths can and should work together in this way. Each religious tradition makes truth claims, and this is of their essence. The doctrinal differences between us, and the necessary consequences of those differences, are essential components of our relationships with one another, making working together both problematic and constantly full of new things to learn. Clarity is essential, and so is experiment and diversity of approach.

And just as there is no single right way for people of different faiths to work together, so there is no single right way for congregations to relate to new and changing communities. In each new situation new ways must be found. Maggie Durran's recent book, *Regenerating Local Churches*, shows this happening, and our book's stories are evidence of a considerable diversity of approach. But this is not to say that a coherent picture doesn't emerge from our book. We think it does, and if it does then it's partly because of the method we used when we wrote it.

As with previous books in this series – *The Parish*, *Diverse Gifts*, and *Ordained Local Ministry* – brief summaries of the chapters were prepared, and then complete drafts. These were circulated to all of the authors, who met for a day to comment on each other's work and to discuss the content of the concluding chapter. Then the chapters were finalized and the Conclusion written. One of the issues we faced was that of repetition. Because all of the authors live in South London, some contexts appear more than once. Where in the same context different perspectives are offered, we have not regarded that as repetition but as useful diversity.

As with the other books, this volume can be read in two ways: as a single book, or as a series of separate essays. So either read it all, or pick out the chapters that relate most closely to those aspects of regeneration and renewal in which you are interested.

Also, as with the other books, this is not an objective survey. It is based in South London (though it also looks more widely on occasion) and it is written on the basis of the authors' own experience and their consultations with others in the places they're writing about and elsewhere. We hope that by writing about our own particular situations, we shall encourage our readers to reflect on *their* own experience, to make links, and to discover and think about differences. We also hope to see new writing from different perspectives.

Just as this exploration makes few claims to objectivity, so also it does not claim to be a theological exploration. It is about what *happens*. Sometimes events and situations give rise to theological reflection within the chapter, but we expect the main theological work to be done by our readers. Our task in this book is to provide some raw material on which others will be able to base their own reflections – and maybe their decisions. One of the reasons for writing this book is to provide a resource for people working in new and changing communities. There are many other good books available, and now particularly *Faithful Cities*, but there is nothing else quite like the records of people's experience contained in these chapters.

We hope that as you relate to the changes going on around you, you will find that what you read here will inform your own ideas and decisions and in particular will enable you to ask about the meaning of 'regeneration'. How are social and spiritual capital related to each other? What is required for genuine human flourishing? How can we promote diversity and yet not create social division? How is the individual's spiritual renewal related to the renewal of places and communities? And you might find yourself asking some more particular questions: What is the relationship between growing consumption and human flourishing? What kind of regeneration is the entertainment industry? How densely should we build new homes? And what has all this got to do with the kingdom of God?

The majority of the contributors to this book are Anglicans, and most of the perspectives are parochial in the sense of being parish-based. It is essential that the different faiths work together in regeneration areas, but it is equally essential that we retain our differences and our distinctiveness. The Christian Church has its own particular revelation, history, faith and action to bring; and the Church of England has *its* own distinctiveness to offer – and that distinctiveness is largely to do with the parish system. Every square inch of this land is in a parish, and within that parish there is a parish church, a congregation and an ordained ministry – and their task is to serve the spiritual needs of the parish as a whole, with 'spiritual' being very broadly defined. It is because of the parish system that the Church of England is deeply involved in new and changing communities, and because of it that changes in the built environment and in communities deeply affect the parish's worship and other activities. If it is to continue to serve new and changing communities effectively, then the Church must treasure its parish system and make it work as hard as it can.

And if the Church is to serve communities with the distinctive gifts that it has to offer, then it must pay attention to its worship and theology. Chapter 3 of *Faith in the City* is an explicitly theological chapter, but interestingly there is no mention of the Eucharist – the taking, giving thanks, breaking and sharing at the heart of Jesus' ministry and of the Church's life. This is surprising as there are many places in the chapter where mention of the Eucharistic nature of the Church's activity and theology would have been both appropriate and productive. (*Faithful Cities*' theological section, §§ 2.50 to 2.69, is equally bereft of discussion of the Eucharist, though there is brief mention elsewhere in the report (§ 7.15).) It is as the Church undertakes these Eucharistic actions that it holds Jesus in remembrance, looks forward to the kingdom of God's completion, becomes the Body of Christ, embodies the kingdom of God, and is inspired to take part in new and diverse forms of faithful action. As *Faithful Cities* puts it:

> The Church 'talks of God' fundamentally and quintessentially in its very activities of offering worship to God, in its life together and its outreach and care for others. In other words, theology takes place most authentically in the very practices of transformative faith-in-action. (§ 2.58)

It is here surely that the second and third definitions of 'regenerate' listed at the beginning of this chapter find their connection. Regeneration of places and communities that result in new and more vigorous life will renew the worship and other action of the Church; regeneration of the Church that results in new and more vigorous life will have an impact on the surrounding community. Both kinds of renewal will change people belonging to both community and Church. In particular, the regeneration of the Church and the community will give a new and higher spiritual nature to members of the Church, and thus to the community in which it is set, for just as no conversion experience or other individual spiritual renewal is without its physical and community effects, so no change in someone's place, community or congregation can fail to affect their spiritual journey. Separating these things is impossible – and the place where their connections are at their clearest is in the Eucharist: in the taking, giving thanks, breaking and sharing that Jesus called us to do.

It is the Church's faithful action that constitutes its spiritual capital and contributes so uniquely to regeneration. This is particularly true of the Church gathering for the Eucharist. The forming of congregations, and their faithful fulfilment of Jesus' command to take bread and wine, give thanks, break bread and share the bread and wine, is thus an essential task of the Church in new and changing communities.

We've called this book *Regeneration and Renewal* for two reasons: first, because among people involved in new and changing communities 'regeneration' now generally refers to change in the built environment, and 'renewal' to the renewal of communities; second, because we hope that our readers will keep in mind the question 'How can we ensure that regeneration results in renewal?'

Further reading

Archbishop's Commission on Urban Priority Areas, *Faith in the City: A Call for Action by Church and Nation*, Church House Publishing, London, 1985.

Commission on Urban Life and Faith, *Faithful Cities: A Call for Celebration, Vision and Justice*, Church House Publishing/Methodist Publishing House, London, 2006.

Durran, M., *Regenerating Local Churches*, Canterbury Press, Norwich, 2006.

Re:New, issue 29, June 2006, Thames Gateway London Partnership.

Torry, M. (ed.), *The Parish: People, Place and Ministry: A Theological and Practical Exploration*, Canterbury Press, Norwich, 2004.

Torry, M. (ed.), *Diverse Gifts: Forms of Ministry in the Church of England*, Canterbury Press, Norwich, 2006.

Torry, M. and Heskins, J. (eds), *Ordained Local Ministry: A New Shape for the Church's Ministry*, Canterbury Press, Norwich, 2006.

Notes

1 The *Oxford English Dictionary* doesn't yet record the recent use of 'regenerate' or 'regeneration' to mean 'to renew the built environment and/or the community of an urban area'. The *Oxford Dictionary of English* (2005) *does* record the new use of 'regeneration' as 'the action or process of regenerating or being regenerated: *the regeneration of inner cities*' (p. 1482). There is currently no information available as to when the words 'regenerate' and 'regeneration' were used specifically of the renewal of urban communities. (I am grateful to Ms Margot Charlton of the Oxford University Press for providing this information on the *Oxford English Dictionary*.)

2 Furbey, R., 'Urban "Regeneration": Reflections on a Metaphor', *Critical Social Policy*, vol. 19, no. 4, 1999, pp. 419–45.

3 *Re:New*, issue 29, June 2006, Thames Gateway London Partnership, p. 7.

2. Regeneration in Southwark

A Political View

JEREMY FRASER

> Then I said to the king, 'If it pleases the king, and if your servant has found favour with you, I ask that you send me to Judah, to the city of my ancestors' graves, so that I may rebuild it.' The king said to me (the queen also was sitting beside him), 'How long will you be gone, and when will you return?' So it pleased the king to send me, and I set him a date. (Nehemiah 2.5, 6)

For 12 years I was a councillor in Southwark.

The council wanted to flatten my Victorian council flat to make way for their latest scheme. I joined the Labour Party to question my councillors, and I became a councillor because I wanted to stop the council making silly decisions. On that basis I failed, but I hope in this chapter to show you the potential for Christians to be involved in decisions about regeneration.

Regeneration isn't a process with defined characteristics, nor does it work with clear parameters. It is a buzz word to package something new that you do not want people to be against. As I have heard it said: it is no good testing the need for change; it should be sufficient that it is regeneration.

I have always been mindful that the process of change disadvantages some people as well as positively helping others. This chapter is not a treatise for taking no action for fear of hurting anyone; rather, it is a plea that there is a price with *any* action. It is no good seeking the greater good without checking the real effect on people.

I shall tell two stories: one about Peckham's estates, and one about unemployment in the London Borough of Southwark. In both cases I shall ask the same questions:

- What is the problem that needs to be overcome?
- Is action really possible?

- Who loses?
- What commitments can be given on the positive outcomes?
- Who judges the outcomes?
- Why are we doing this?
- Did it work?

Peckham

What is the problem?

The five estates of North Peckham is an area equivalent to a whole council ward, and they were so intertwined that it was said that you could walk between the blocks without ever going to the ground. The aim was to make pedestrian-safe areas, to create better homes for people formerly living in crowded conditions, to make new communities. The vision was not wrong. Much of the housing that the estates replaced was slums, and the indoor toilets and bathrooms in the new dwellings were a real improvement. But the flats had been designed and built without reference to the blocks similarly built earlier in Chicago and elsewhere that had already become areas where people did not want to live.

These areas did not attract or hold on to people with any choice as to where they lived. I give some colourful statistics of the area that impressed upon me that the sticking-plaster approach of my predecessors had not worked – and would not work. Some 27 per cent of children of school age had no adult in their family in work over two generations. This was at a time of 11 per cent unemployment nationally and 15 per cent locally. This was a place where you had no options, and no role models for staying on in education. Drugs were rife and teenage pregnancies among the highest in the country. This self-perpetuating cycle was not just saddening; it was leading to a ten-year-plus life expectancy lower than on neighbouring estates and communities.

The estates' crime levels were enormous. British Gas would only go on to the estates in threes: the person doing the repair; someone to help them; and someone to be locked in the van to protect the van and equipment.

Was action really possible?

My daughter was six months old and I was with a group of mums (I was the only man). We were in the health clinic which formed part of the Peckham estates. The people there were guarded in front of someone they did not know, but as we waited our turn for weighing and talking to the health visitor, the conversation started.

The mums started to talk about the fact that the council was again going to discuss whether they could pull down the estates and build new homes. They knew it was soon because of the consultation. What they were unsure of was when the meeting was going to be (that night) and they did not know that I was the leader of the council.

The conversation was fatalistic: the council won't do anything, can't do anything. The conversation appeared to reach a consensus: 'There are downsides to any change, but radical change is needed now. Sadly the council will not have the courage to face down those against it and make it happen.' I believe that God puts us into certain places, and that day was one of those. The frustrating public meetings regarding the future of the estate (which these women had no wish to attend) were steered by those on the estate opposed to the change; it was a moan about the council. The opposition went something like: 'If you can't fix my damp/window/intercom or get me a transfer, why should I trust you to deliver a project so large we will all be affected?' It was a very reasonable point. The council was both the largest English landlord and also had one of the lowest customer satisfaction ratings.

It would be easier to do something nice like plant a tree or open a nursery, so why did I sit in public meetings getting abuse thrown at me? Basically, because the tenants, and especially those opposed to radical change, were right. Would I trust someone who had never undertaken something so big – meaning that no one on the council had any experience of how to do it and would therefore be at the mercy of external professionals. Clearly, I could only engender trust by getting small problems solved where I could. When I was leader of the council I did ten surgeries a month. There is nothing more effective at finding out what we are doing wrong than listening to those who are aggrieved. Many times I discovered something that others in the organization felt I did not need to know.

The catharsis of the meetings allowed us to move towards smaller planning meetings, with tenants electing representatives to plan the options. I asked those fundamentally opposed to constructively take part (this did not always work). The peer pressure generally kept it moving forward. Those mums were not represented by me or their tenants' associations, because they felt that the process was too complex. They disengaged and awaited their fate.

I went to the crucial evening meeting fired up to make sure the decisions were made. All the consultation the council had done had been inconclusive: overall in favour of the change but not unanimous; and the tenants opposed to change were always louder than those in favour. But those mums, members of the silent majority of the estate, had made a deep impression on me.

Around a table, we debated as a small group of councillors with the tenants' representatives. Just prior to the meeting the opposition leader had stopped me in the corridor and pledged his vote for a regeneration process at the end of the night. 'I will give you a hard time and press the case of those concerns, but you will have a cross party decision,' he stated.

Those at the meeting knew that action had been taken of a limited kind – blocking walkways and redesigning blocks to make them more secure – but that the problems had not disappeared. We debated, had walk-outs by tenants, and amendments by the opposition. We talked from 7 p.m. until 2 a.m., but by then we had a decision: a recommendation to go forward.

Who loses?

The tenure of the housing would need to change; the council could not be the new landlord. An irony was that those who came to rubbish the idea of the council being able to do a regeneration project when they could not mend a broken window still preferred the council as landlord.

The democratic link of electoral accountability was something they thought they would lose. The ability to visit the town hall and actually talk to your landlord feels right. Despite the failure of this council ward to serve its tenants, the estate had been Labour since it was built, and for 50 years before that. One result of impending regeneration was a lower election turnout one year, the lowest turnout of a ward in England. The two real issues relating to wanting to stay with the council as landlord were the stronger tenancy laws when compared with a new tenancy under another social housing provider, and less control of rent increases with a new landlord. The government had at various times suggested that subsidy should be cut and housing associations might be required to make a return on their investment (a social profit); therefore, the rental levels would change and residents would pay more for smaller units and a less strong tenure.

There was a significant number of people who had illegally sub-let their property, although there was an annual check that tenants were still in residence. This was meant to weed out people who had moved away and rented out their flat to a person who might not otherwise be eligible for housing from the council. About 10 per cent of the flats were vacated without the council having to re-house the residents. The people who were on the margins, and possibly not legally resident in the UK, tended to disappear, although we did advertise the advice centres that could assist them. The next 'losers' had already lost quite a bit and, just as it looked as if the corner was being turned, they felt that they would lose even more. These were the leaseholders. They had exercised the right to buy and bought a flat (quite cheaply) both as an investment (sic) and as a commitment to the area. They were now in negative equity. These losers were clear about what they wanted. We found a number of similar properties in the surrounding area that were of the same value. We then swapped the flats. It seemed to be the only way to avoid the leaseholder having to pay to get out of their flats. (The irony was that the council was the leaseholders' original mortgage lender, so could have required the full mortgage repayment for a council flat that was now worth less than when the leaseholder bought it from the council.)

Commitments given

It was important to set down an open list of commitments that the council could keep to. This is something I use today (I am currently involved in about 30 regeneration schemes across London). It is not about offering silly things, but about listening to what the main concerns are and seeing what honest responses can be made.

A lot of residents wanted to return, and the number increased as the new housing started to appear – and we kept our word that all who wanted to return could do so. Previously when people were moved to other housing to make way for a development, most stayed in the housing they had moved into rather than move back. This did not happen. This time people came back.

We helped to keep children at their existing schools, and enabled all other normal links to be maintained. An understanding about rents was reached with the housing associations. We also did two things you might not expect. We allowed original residents to be the first to buy or part-buy a flat in the area, and gardening classes were organized. People had no memory of a garden, and now most families had their own back garden and wanted to learn how to look after it.

What we failed to do very well involved the decanting of the blocks of flats. As soon as you start to empty a block it is vulnerable to vandalism and squatters, and arson becomes a problem. We tried to learn and do it better than before, but it was an area we were not prepared for. It was in one of the transient areas that Damilola Taylor died.

Who judges the outcome?

Well, to be honest, just about everyone. The tenants themselves, obviously. And the verdict? It isn't perfect, far from it, but the area has changed. It is no longer a place to film the gritty scenes of TV dramas such as *The Bill*; instead, it has hosted garden and interior design makeover film crews. The council themselves, the Audit Commission, the government, and the housing corporation all had reports written on the project and its outcomes. The lesson of the errors made is available for all to read and, hopefully, *is* read before other major schemes are planned.

Employment

What is the problem?

The second regeneration scenario I want to discuss is the chronic unemployment that I found in parts of the borough. The solution had been to build industrial sheds near to the large estates and hope that employment would appear. Since the nearby docks had closed, no large employers other than Price Waterhouse had moved into the area. The borough's largest employers were the council, the NHS, and the colleges and schools. We had, at the point I took over as leader, a training place for every adult in the borough (the fact that they were either not taken up or were taken up by people from other areas appeared irrelevant). Even the units used were very light on employment as they had become storage areas for the centre of London. This was not in itself bad, but it was not an answer to unemployment. The city was meanwhile experiencing a boom and the West End was full of tourists. The question therefore was why Southwark people were not getting more of those jobs, and whether this was just a by-product of the economic cycle?

As a politician at that time, I saw the problem as solvable. It wasn't a matter of 'the poor will always be with you', nor a straight anti-capitalist view of society, for this problem was clearly linked to that of the run-down estates. The two issues had been live for at least the four previous leaders of the council. They had all, within the Tory government's constraints, tried options to solve the two problems of the Peckham estates and unemployment. None had pretended the problems did not exist, but had perhaps accepted that progress would be difficult, if not impossible, particularly in relation to unemployment.

Is action really possible?

If Norman Tebbit was to be believed, unemployment was because of people's idleness and inability to get on their collective 'bikes'. I found it a rather more complex issue (sorry, Norman). The lack of role models and confidence had caused people to be in a false comfort zone of 'there is nothing in life for me'. This opt-out was frankly scary, as a few years before we had had riots. How could vision be restored?

Studies pointed to jobs being there, but with people unable or unwilling to access them. I found people regularly telling me that they could not remember when they had crossed the river into the City or West End for any reason. They viewed it as somewhere that was not for them. Jobs were not appearing locally, but there were lots just a short bus ride away. The neighbouring boroughs were supportive. The City Corporation under Michael Cassidy had decided that the isolationist approach of the Corporation was unacceptable. They did not wish to see the City's expansion threatened by the failure of the neighbouring boroughs to start to confront their issues. He was, and is, very socially aware. Miles Young in the City of Westminster was similar and had offered help. Neither of these men were socialists, but politics is about delivery, and if these people would help me to deliver a better future for Southwark, then I should listen.

John Gummer MP, the then Secretary of State for the Environment, was supportive, but frankly, like those tenants on the Peckham estates, did not believe that the council knew how to deliver. He suggested a partnership between four boroughs to spend government money and to exchange advice and help. Lambeth was included.

The first meeting was arranged and Michael Cassidy called me in the morning before the meeting and told me that Lambeth was hung and had no agreed leader, and that he did not want to support Westminster. He said that I had his support for a radical programme of regenerating the north bank of Southwark and Lambeth, and linking the area to the jobs and opportunities in the two cities. I felt vindicated in trying to make a new relationship with the City. About an hour later Miles Young rang, saying almost exactly the same as Michael, except that he did not trust the Corporation. The day came and the three of us awaited the Lambeth representative. The three party leaders from Lambeth turned up and were immediately sent outside by us to choose one leader to join us. The structure of getting cash together and a method of getting change to happen now seemed possible. Cross-river partnership was born, working with employers and those who want a job. It has created thousands of opportunities. It has also created a lot of physical infrastructure to help link the banks of the Thames (two bridges, a river-boat service including piers, bus interchanges, new bus routes, and now a tram route).

Who loses?

The losers were those who found their area changing and being less homogeneous. Changes in the Bankside area had raised house prices and pushed the original residents out, and they had been replaced by absentee landlords and people moving in for brief periods. The new residents were less likely to use the area as their only residence, and were unlikely to use many services or bring up children in Southwark. The community has become similar to many other parts of the inner London area and this had an effect on schools and services. Before the Tate Modern gallery was announced, a neighbouring council estate (the last council housing built by the council, completed about 1986) called me to one of their meetings. People complained that the area was dead and there was nowhere for them to shop. They said that they had been dumped there and wanted to move out. I asked for about six months and said that I thought that the area would change in that time. (I did not know how much.) They did not call me back. The Tate Modern and the Borough Market changed everything. (The Borough Market was a historic charter fruit and vegetable market which was only open for a couple of hours each night to service the restaurant trade. It became a full-time premium place to buy high-quality food.) The residents still find problems with the lack of ordinary local shops (another problem of rising land values pushing out cheap shops and making space too expensive for a supermarket). Those losers have not lost more than they had lost already, and the gain they made was in house prices and the general feeling of the area.

Commitments given

Here the tasks were more aspirational and in a sense easier. We gave commitments on training and employment and on new facilities in the area. We promised to look at the barriers to change and to find ways around them. Pecan, a Christian charity, offered support and training. Some council officers were nervous about an overtly Christian group leading employment support in Peckham and spearheading the project to prepare people for the new jobs. My Christian faith was reasonably well known and I asked whether anyone else would undertake the work at the level they operated at, or at the price they asked? 'No one' was the reply.

Pecan were visiting people in their homes, explaining the process, supporting people with the issues that stood in the way of training, getting children into nurseries, accessing benefits, etc. They then committed to continue to visit and, if need be, actually go with the resident to the training base. This was a truly Christian approach to valuing people. And British Gas helped too. People were promised interviews and support after training until they got a job.

Who judges the outcome?

The employment climate has changed, but what I enjoy most are the stories the Cross River Partnership (the four borough partnership described above) publishes of local people, for local people are good at telling what has happened since the intervention. Not just jobs in Bankside and the South Bank, but support to access employment across the capital. The funding was largely government and European. The Partnership still exists and is promoting among other things a tramway through three of the four boroughs. Most other such partnerships have disappeared as the funding dried up. Cross River, though, is still seen as relevant, and it has received new funding from a number of sources.

Why are you doing this?

It might seem odd that this is put so late in this account, but I wanted to tell the two stories before trying to make some overall points that might help churches as they find themselves in a regeneration area.

The first question a faith group puts to whoever is promoting a scheme is 'why?' Let us not be naïve. There are more schemes planned than actually happen, and what matters is how real the chances are of the project happening. Watch out for the timetable slipping. I have seen schemes take years longer in the planning, with nothing actually happening – and, because of the large regeneration idea, normal small things don't happen. Shops don't get re-let, repairs don't happen, houses get boarded up – with all the accompanying risk of vandalism and the area being pushed further down.

Sometimes a failure to solve a small problem can encourage local government to try something more grand. It may not be achievable, but if it might get them past the coming election, then they promise and publicize it.

I remember asking an officer why, after all the regeneration that was happening in one area, the shops were still boarded up and not looking inviting. We discovered that the council had, some 20 years before, bought parts of the sites for a road widening that thankfully was now never going to happen. Our ownership was stopping investment in the shops – right next door to our fancy posters and bold statements. It was very embarrassing, and while others had not noticed it, this was a humbling lesson that helped us to get the council's own house in order.

Did it work?

The area is better for the intervention, but perhaps the real test is in ten years' time (especially if there is an economic downturn).

Change disadvantages some people. Some people are stranded in the area, they cannot move (the council is their landlord), and they feel that they have no voice and no hope. But this chapter is not a manifesto for no action out of fear of hurting someone, but rather a statement that there is a price to any action. It is into this space that the Christian fits. Standing with those done to. Not protesting all the time, but picking the issues and bringing God's kingdom closer on earth.

At the beginning, the church people who prayed and supported were personally a great support. And these were the church people who wanted justice, helped local residents to manage the consultation, and then picked up the pieces.

Regeneration might be a buzz word created by lazy bureaucrats, but we can make it into something good for our communities.

Further reading

Hinchliff, P., *Holiness and Politics*, Darton, Longman and Todd, London, 1982.

3. Knowing the Facts

The Church's Collection of the Information It Needs

CATRIONA ROBERTSON

In the twenty-fifth year of our exile, at the beginning of the year, on the tenth day of the month, in the fourteenth year after the city was struck down, on that very day, the hand of the LORD was upon me, and he brought me there. He brought me, in visions of God, to the land of Israel, and set me down upon a very high mountain, on which was a structure like a city to the south. When he brought me there, a man was there, whose appearance shone like bronze, with a linen cord and a measuring reed in his hand; and he was standing in the gateway. (Ezekiel 40.1–3)

In 2001, faced with a bewildering array of regeneration initiatives, Anglicans in London South Central decided to get up to speed with what was going on and what was being planned. With giant cranes heralding the arrival of new office blocks and luxury flats, local authorities consulting on the transfer of their estates to housing associations and a myriad of health, employment and educational schemes in the pipeline, how could the parish churches plan to serve a residential population that could change out of all recognition within a decade? They joined forces with churches from other denominations and with people of other faiths and commissioned a piece of research work. I had conducted a couple of social audits for churches in South London, so I put in a tender for the work and won the contract.

This chapter tells the story of how the faith communities and I found the information we needed, how we made sense of it, and how we found a way for the Church to play an authentic and distinctive role within layers of complex and fast-moving government and private-sector initiatives in an area that had already experienced a great deal of change.

Regeneration in London South Central

The four main tasks of the six-month project were:

- To understand the needs of local people.
- To map current and future regeneration activity.
- To document the work of faith communities.
- To explore possible responses by faith communities to expected changes in the area.

In retrospect, it was hugely ambitious. None of us was aware of any comparable work on a similar scale. The lead player, Southwark and Newington Deanery, and the then rural dean, Canon Grahame Shaw, were highly enthusiastic and had convinced a number of individuals and grant-making bodies to fund the work. As a member of a community-oriented Anglican parish church not far from the project area, I was as keen as the project's Steering Group to find out what was going on and to encourage the church to consider how best to respond. A few meetings later, Steering Group members and the then diocesan community development adviser, Jill McKinnon, had shared useful ideas and documents with me and given me the contact details of a few key people. It was a good working relationship from the start.

Seeing is believing: maps

London South Central is the quarter of central London that lies south of the River Thames. I was given a street map of the project area: it straddled two London boroughs (Southwark and Lambeth) and included the Elephant and Castle and the sweep of riverside from Vauxhall to Tower Bridge. My first task was to find a better-quality map. At Stanfords, the map suppliers in Covent Garden, I found a clear, detailed, super-scale map of the project area. I also looked at some historical documents, including Charles Booth's 1889 *London Map of Poverty*. Later I picked up a selection of inner-London maps and guides. Between them, they provided a good range of information on places of worship, schools, visitor attractions, hospitals, railway lines, shopping centres, cultural and arts venues, universities and parks. I planned to mark the information I collected myself (for example, regeneration activity, location of faith communities, parish boundaries, social housing) on clear acetate sheets and bind the final report in such a way as to allow readers to choose which acetates, or combination of acetates, to view over the master map. In this way they would be able to see exactly what was going on in each part of the project area and be able to pinpoint their own particular patch. The text of the report would be useful for some, but I was hoping that the maps would provide plenty of information, and that on the maps the patterns would be easy to spot and the connections easier to make.

After obtaining permission to reproduce the master map, and registering under the Data Protection Act, I was ready to go in search of the information I needed. I quickly accumulated a large selection of books, reports, ward profiles, papers from the Mayor of London's office, statutory and voluntary-sector publications, local government plans and consultation exercises, and a wealth of literature from the regeneration professionals themselves.

Avoiding the continuous present: history

A little research revealed the fascinating story of a part of London that for a long time lay outside the boundaries and was associated with the less acceptable aspects of city life: poverty, crime, illness, prisons, bad housing, and fragile mental health. The work available to local people was mostly in polluting industries such as tanning, brewing and hat-making. You do not have to dig very deep to find heavily contaminated soil left behind from the pottery trade, but popular entertainment and theatre thrived, it was the starting point for pilgrimages, and there was a well-developed tradition of asylum. From Roman times, London South Central has had a diverse population, welcoming people first from European countries and then from further afield, the changing pattern often echoing events abroad.

From the start, pioneering work undertaken by religious orders, parishes – and later the settlements and missions as well – helped to lead the way in lessening the suffering of those trapped in poverty, poor housing, unemployment, illiteracy and ill health. Religious orders, parishes and voluntary initiatives built hospitals and affordable housing, started schools and evening classes for the less well-off, and created accessible centres of excellence for the performing arts. Many of the settlements – progressive communities where rich and poor, educated and unschooled lived together to forge a common life – are still, in evolved forms, in existence today, and St Thomas's and Guy's Hospitals, Octavia Hill's housing, Emma Cons's and Lilian Bayliss's Old Vic and Morley College, as well as the many church schools in the area, remind us of the commitment of past generations of Christians.

As the research progressed, it became clear that many of these historical threads were still in evidence. The two Roman roads were still straight, and Black Prince Road still belonged to the Duchy of Cornwall. Booth's colour-coded Map of Poverty showed the richest houses lining the major roads, with the worst poverty tucked away out of sight behind them. In 2002, the tall Georgian houses on Kennington Road were popular with MPs as they fell within the Division Bell area for the House of Commons. A few steps to the west, however, towards the river and towards Lambeth Palace, brought you to the Ethelred Estate which still has 'a high proportion of severely deprived households' according to the latest statistics. Poor-quality homes and the lack of affordable housing – and what to do about it – were hot issues. There were high levels of crime and mental ill health. The area was one of the most ethnically diverse in the country. Refugees from the Irish potato famine had followed the earlier Germans, Dutch and Flemings, and had in turn given way to the Windrush generation of migrant workers from the Caribbean, the asylum-seekers from Kosovo and Colombia, and Nigerian, Ghanaian, Middle Eastern and South Asian families, all joining previous newcomers and the white working class, professionals and celebrities in the area.

Around the time of the research, popular entertainment and the arts were blossoming, with the opening of the Tate Modern art gallery, the Imax cinema at Waterloo, Shakespeare's Globe, the redevelopment of the Royal Festival Hall, and the continued popularity of the National Theatre and National Film Theatre.

Two events during the twentieth century, however, continued to have a marked impact on the area. First, the destruction of large areas by bombing during World War Two resulted in nearly 10,000 new homes being built by 1955 and the Elephant and Castle area being redeveloped during the 1960s. Second, the area suffered a dramatic drop in employment during the 1970s and early 1980s when the docks and much of the manufacturing industry closed down or moved away.

History matters. It's hard to peer into the future with any confidence without some grasp of the past. Regeneration activity has a reputation in some quarters for short-term thinking and the pursuit of quick wins, but the faith communities take a far longer view over the centuries than the usual three-, seven- or ten-year project. Initiatives come and go, but the Church, on the whole, stays present and engaged. The Church had been instrumental in much previous regeneration work, but were the churches and other faith communities still bothered by the stark inequalities evident in the lives of local people? Were they responding to what they found, speaking out on injustice, engaged in supporting those who had fallen on hard times? We needed to find out exactly what the local needs were, how the regeneration schemes were planning to meet them, and what kind of community work the faith communities were involved in. A combination of statistics, interviews with local workers, questionnaires and vox pops surveys combined to provide a snapshot of what was going on.

Getting the facts right: statistics, boundaries, indicators and figures

Population

With the results of the 2001 Census not yet available and the 1991 Census figures considerably out of date, other sources of demographic statistics had to be found. It took a while to be confident that the figures I eventually used for the estimated number of residents, their age profile, and their ethnic groups, were acceptable. The London Research Centre, the Government Actuary's Office and the local health authority were all useful sources, but projections from earlier figures were unavoidable. It took time to piece together statistics from two boroughs, matching age and ethnicity groupings and finding the appropriate London and national comparators (or rather, English and Welsh comparators, since Scottish and Northern Irish figures are collected separately). Irritatingly, all they confirmed was that the population was young, ethnically diverse and had about the same proportion of males to females – as anyone at a bus stop at the Elephant and Castle could have told you. It is now very much easier to pin down the figures you need (including religious affiliation) from the National Statistics website.

Deprivation

The word 'poverty' seems to have slipped out of the national conversation and, when it *is* used, is often hedged about with qualifications. 'Deprivation' is the favoured term and the Indices of Multiple Deprivation (IMD) 2000, a government set of figures from a variety of sources, were intended to be a useful way of comparing the deprivation of residents of small areas (electoral wards) in different parts of the country. There were 8,414 wards in England and Wales in 2000, with the most deprived ward ranked first in the IMD and the least deprived coming last at number 8,414.

Seven out of the twelve wards in London South Central fell within the most deprived 10 per cent of wards in England and Wales, which was the criterion then used by the Church Urban Fund to identify a ward as a priority area for action and funding. The remaining wards were not much better off and the close juxtaposition of deprivation and affluence in the area suggested that pockets of even greater poverty existed, offset in the statistics of the better-off areas nearby. The recent introduction of statistics for much smaller areas – Lower Layer Super Output Areas – has eased this problem.

The Child Poverty Index showed the percentage of children living in families on a low income: for example, those on benefits. The average score across the area was 50 per cent. More recently, there has been considerable concern about the number of families who have 'no recourse to public funds' and are therefore ineligible for state benefits, but in 2002 those living on benefits, especially for long periods of time, were considered to be struggling the most.

So, half the children in London South Central were living in poverty and much of the area was considered to fall within the most deprived 10 per cent in the country. I included in the report some observations I made while interviewing. Inner-city people can lose their critical edge and become acclimatized to what is normal: doctors become used to high rates of depression among their patients; schools get used to a high turnover of staff and supply teachers; we stop noticing the iron grilles across the front doors on some estates; we forget that the purpose of making anything 'exclusive' is to exclude.

Crime

Crime figures were not as freely available as they are now that the Metropolitan Police has made substantial efforts to ensure that we can all track levels of crime in our own area through websites and bulletins such as *Communities Together*, but back then I had to rely on borough Crime and Disorder Audits and on Community Safety Strategies, and from these I was able to find the crime hotspots in the project area and to see what trends there were within a fluctuating set of figures. HM Inspectorate of Constabulary said that Lambeth was one of the most challenging policing environments in the UK – and possibly even in Europe. Southwark's figures showed similar increases in street crime to Lambeth, and hotspots occurred where larger numbers of people gather: at public transport interchanges and in shopping areas.

I counted the yellow witness appeal boards on the pavements and I looked for the bin chamber where a murder victim had been found. Both the police and local residents were unsurprised at the level of violence. Viewing the busy and beautiful riverside from a police launch on the Thames one sunny March morning, it was tempting to forget the fear and grief that crime leaves in its wake.

Looking at the priorities for reducing crime in each borough in 2002, I noticed that 'hate' crime did not include 'faith hate' crime, which is nowadays monitored very closely.

Employment

Lack of employment is closely linked to poverty, especially in the long term. With so much building work in progress and new employers moving in, there was a reasonable hope that new opportunities would become available for unemployed residents. The figures from Labour Market Statistics showed the two boroughs to have high Claimant Counts (one of the measures of unemployment). Lambeth's Claimant Count rate in April 2002 was over twice the UK and Greater London averages.

The figures on their own, although informative, seemed a bit dry. How did they connect to real people? I contacted the London Bridge office of the Southwark Employment Service, which was just about to metamorphose into a three-borough JobCentre Plus. Talking to one of the managers, I found that the largest employers in the project area were the big hospitals, followed by the two local authorities, and then the retail sector. Building and construction work was likely to offer the most opportunity in the short to medium term, as More London (the site of the new Mayor's office) and other sites were developed. Catering and jobs in tourism along the riverside were usually filled casually. A gap was evident between the skills necessary for the office work becoming available and the existing skills of local would-be employees. I talked to unemployed people leaving the Newington Causeway Job Centre. They liked the central location and the good public transport, but felt the area was run down and violent. Racial discrimination was felt keenly when it came to jobs at managerial level, and they thought that faith communities could do more to educate people on diversity and to support people in difficulty.

More recent work of mine in Peckham in 2006 highlighted the added competition for jobs from Eastern Europeans from countries such as Poland and Lithuania which joined the EU in 2004. These economic migrants are often young, healthy, highly motivated and attractive to employers, in contrast to the local unskilled long-term unemployed population. Most of these economic migrants have entered the country legally, but there is a sizeable number of 'irregular migrants' (contract cleaners, home carers, food processing workers) without whom, it has been reported, London would find it hard to function. But in 2002, it was mainly competition from within the UK that jeopardized the availability of jobs available to residents of London South Central. Buses from the north-east of England, itself an area of high unemployment, were bringing men down to work on construction sites, putting them up in bunkhouses from Monday to Thursday and bussing them home again on Friday after work.

High hopes for employment opportunities from the 2012 Olympic Games construction sites have already reached Lambeth, but ensuring new local jobs go to local people is not always so easy – and the justice issues for the Church and other faith communities, which have a local presence not only in the north-east of England but in Poland, Lithuania, Colombia and the Balkans, are not as straightforward as might at first appear. Should we not care as much about employment for Eastern Europeans as we do for Londoners? It was clear that global and local met on a regular basis in London South Central.

Tourism

The riverside area of London South Central was and is a tourist magnet. British Airways' London Eye and Tate Modern ranked third and fourth as London's most visited attractions. Even the events of 11 September 2001 had only reduced overseas visitor spending by 14 per cent. Over seven million people visit London South Central each year – or rather, they visit the riverside area. My sketch maps were beginning to take shape. Noting the location of the tourist attractions highlighted the fact that most of this activity took place between the elevated railway line (which runs through Vauxhall, Waterloo and London Bridge) and the river. Rather like the old British maps, the pink bits (in this case denoting visitor attractions and cultural venues) on my super-scale map were to be found, with one exception, along this narrow strip. Presumably much of the investment and spending, therefore, was within this area too. I spent Easter Day on vox pop surveys of the happy crowds along the riverside walk. The only pink rectangle on my map outside this area was the Imperial War Museum. Those in the know pointed out that the river was a useful orientation landmark and that visitors to the Museum had to make a special effort to venture 'inland'. Sure enough, the crowds evaporated as I walked away from the river. This pattern was to become more significant as the research progressed.

Education

It was relatively easy to get hold of the school league tables (then in paper form, now only available online) and to find the main statistics. Over a third of the primary and nearly half of the secondary schools were Church of England or Roman Catholic schools. Nearly half of the children qualified for free school meals (often used as a proxy for low income), up to a third spoke a language other than English at home, and nearly half had special educational needs. Unsurprisingly, although some schools (particularly the church schools) were doing well, the performance tables showed many of the children performing below average. Three of the seven secondary schools bumped along the bottom of the graph. As ever, the figures did not depict the whole story: not all of the pupils attending schools in the area were local (some came from as far away as Herne Hill), but there was no residential postcode analysis of academic achievement. There were far fewer secondary school places than primary places, and with no explanation for this offered by either of the two education authorities the assumption had to be that parents sent their children to schools out of the borough or educated them privately. Anecdotal evidence (confirmed to some extent by new academic research) suggested that parents, where possible, did not want to send their children to schools that were perceived to be failing. They were prepared to move house or pay for private schooling to achieve this, with resulting knock-on effects on the local area.

Health

Wholeness, healing, and living life to the full, are values shared by the main world faiths. The people living in the project area had higher infant mortality, died earlier, and had higher rates of mental ill health, sexually transmitted infections and teenage pregnancy than people living in almost all other areas of England and Wales. Some of the figures that floated off innocuous-looking grids were shocking and I had to check that I had not made a stupid error: schizophrenia was over three times the national average; 15 per cent of children were estimated to have major mental health problems (not minor ones); the secure ward population (for those suffering the most acute mental illness) from black and minority ethnic groups was a highly disproportionate 60 per cent. There was a shortage of GPs and interpretation services, Accident and Emergency Units were being used by people who should really have gone to their GP, and treatment for serious illnesses was beginning later than it ought to have done as a result of an unwillingness to visit the surgery.

However, the Sure Start and New Pin programmes were getting going and had already made a positive impact, attracting vulnerable young parents and helping them to look after their babies.

Housing

People need places to live, so housing becomes a critical factor in community life. The 'right to buy' legislation in 1980 had a profound effect on local authorities' ability to provide social housing, leaving the Registered Social Landlords (RSLs) to take responsibility for it. The legislation also had the effect of introducing a greater mix to council estates. A combination of 'right to buy' and 'buy to let' trends was resulting in students and flat-sharers living on council estates. Extended family networks were broken up when people who were brought up on council estates were neither eligible for their own council flat nor able to afford a mortgage for even the cheapest local flat on the open market. There was very little social housing marked on my sketch map along the riverside, but large estates covered much of the 'interior'. Many of these properties were in poor repair, with few facilities provided for residents.

The private sector, in contrast, had been attracted to the narrow strip between the river and the elevated railway line, and developers were building large, luxury, gated blocks of flats. I wondered why the smaller developments often had exactly 14 apartments. I later learned that any development over that number brought with it an obligation under the 'planning gain' policy, by which a varying proportion of the residential units has to be made available at affordable prices or a financial contribution made to the local authority to be used for the benefit of the community. Opinions varied as to whether raising the 'planning gain' percentage would bring more affordable housing or simply put developers off. Land and property values in the project area were high: the smallest flat commanded a six-figure sum and the new riverside apartments were going for over a million pounds each. In the Bermondsey and London Bridge area old industrial buildings, such as tanneries and a jam factory, were being converted into flats, giving the parents of better-off students at Guy's Medical School the opportunity to house their children and sell at a profit after graduation.

The acute shortage of housing in the south-east of England, very high land and property values in the project area, and the lack of funds for maintaining council property, combined to create a polar-ized picture of housing, with an effect all too familiar in inner-city areas: luxury accommodation for those who could afford it along the riverside, poor-quality social housing for those who qualified, and very little in between. Nurses, teachers and police officers did not earn enough to buy property and usually had to commute in from outer London. Cleaners, hospital porters and care workers earned even less.

My research took place at a time when council tenants and lease-holders on two major estates (Aylesbury and Ethelred) were being offered a choice: keep the council as your landlord and continue to see limited property maintenance, or agree formally to the transfer of the housing stock to an RSL and see it either replaced with better-quality housing or renovated to a high standard. Local activists and politicians from further afield joined the campaigns for and against. Both estates voted against stock transfer. It seems that consultation was not as full as it could have been and that the residents were not sufficiently convinced that the advantages (better-quality homes) outweighed the potential disadvantages (higher rents in the longer term and less accountability by the RSLs, who might have to answer to banks rather than the ballot box if they fell into financial difficulty). Redevelopment of the Heygate estate at the Elephant and Castle was also controversial: the estate was poorly designed and in need of substantial repair or replacement, but residents would have to be moved out of the area, temporarily or permanently, for this to happen. My own view, after talking to residents on several estates, was that there was a fair degree of scepticism directed towards the people giving out glossy leaflets and promising a rosy future. For people with little else, the home is very precious and not something to take unnecessary risks over.

Who really knows what's going on? The regeneration maze

Regeneration schemes, possibly because they carry so many hopes but maybe also because very large amounts of money are usually involved, seem to be unusually difficult to find out about. My immediate challenge was first to decide what initiatives counted as regeneration, then to find them all and, finally, to add their area of operation to my map. I had assumed that someone, somewhere, would have a list, possibly accompanied by a map, a short para-graph on what each initiative was expected to achieve, and a list of contacts. When I discovered that this was not the case I attempted to compile one myself. This task was never completed to my satisfac-tion. I was very surprised, and rather relieved, at my launch event, to find local government officers rushing up to me and exclaiming that I had 'put it all together' for them. Until then they had never really understood the bigger picture.

By 2002, the word 'regeneration', a hopeful word for Christians, was going out of fashion: the 'Urban Renaissance' of the 2000 Urban White Paper and the Social Exclusion Unit's 'Neighbourhood Renewal' of 2001 were edging in. Even defining 'regeneration' was controversial: some thought it was a synonym for gentrification; others included or excluded private investment. Most were agreed that regeneration must lead to benefits, but debate continued to centre on who the real beneficiaries were. In my report I included any plans to develop the built environment, and any projects, schemes and initiatives that aimed to improve the lives of local residents.

The language associated with regeneration had warranted the publication of a booklet entitled *The Regeneration Maze* (now re-issued as *The Regeneration Maze Revisited*) and several jargon-busters explained the difference between an 'output' and an 'outcome'. There has been little improvement since. If you do not know about Local Area Agreements, 'stretch targets', Practice Based Commissioning and Safer Neighbourhoods, in 2007 you are not considered to be a serious player. The rhetoric around regeneration is full of references to inclusion, involvement, empowerment and community, but as I talked to local people in London South Central I found that the people who were involved in the regeneration process (often unfairly labelled 'the usual suspects') found it all extremely time-consuming, and those who were not were thoroughly confused. The frequency with which boundaries, funding streams, geographical areas of responsibility and even government departments altered was also disconcerting. Ward boundaries and names changed in 2002. Primary Care Trusts were just starting up, Community Health Councils were closing down. New Deal for Communities was entering its uncertain period and Single Regeneration Budgets were being phased out. We were trying to find out what a 'floor target' was and what the Mayor of London's 'functional bodies' were. City Hall was not yet built and people gazed at the artist's impression of the More London site on the hoardings, wondering whether all these glassy buildings would actually appear.

I wondered the same thing and spoke to people from the planning departments in both boroughs. When planning permission is granted it is no guarantee that the scheme will go ahead – so examining the Unitary Development Plans and finding out what permissions had been given did not provide me with a definite picture of London South Central in a few years' time. I tried to make an educated guess from reading between the lines of my interviewees. My map quickly acquired a mass of anticipated private sector housing and office construction, transport interchanges, new social housing and government offices.

The areas covered by the major regeneration partnerships included most of the map: around the riverside they overlapped more than once, and in the 'interior' there were two gaps, but between them they pretty much covered the whole area. Smaller partnerships such as Health Action Zones, basic-skills projects, credit unions, Town Centre Management offices, smoking-cessation projects, and teenage pregnancy-prevention schemes were also active, boosting educational achievement, improving employment prospects, reducing crime and increasing the capacity of community groups. The Cross-River Partnership was encouraging local people to take up the new job opportunities.

Much of the anticipated riverside development has taken place as planned, but the transformation of the Elephant and Castle area has yet to materialize. Ribbon redevelopment led away from the bridges towards the Elephant and Castle, and the hope was that once that area was revitalized the trend would continue further south and east to Walworth, Camberwell and Peckham. Looking at the map, it was clear that without investment in the Elephant and Castle, it was likely that the 'interior' would continue to struggle and could be left behind while the riverside went from strength to strength. The Waterloo area had a longer history of regeneration (in which the Festival of Britain in 1951 was an important element), a co-ordinated business network, active residential and faith communities, and spare space (for example, car-parks) for building development, and was moving forward at a steady pace. The Elephant and Castle plans involved a close interlocking of major infrastructure and other projects, so it was harder to go ahead with one aspect without affecting the outcome of the others. The lack of space meant that new housing could not be built without demolishing old housing. There had been no lack of consultation in the area (over 60 surveys), but, with very little yet to see in return, local people were becoming wary. There were suspicions that the push for regeneration and new housing could be aimed at relocating low-income residents and opening the area up for wealthier residents. This would have the effect of reducing the incidence of deprivation in the area by displacing it rather than eliminating it. Others worried that an already divided society was becoming more polarized: those who could afford the new flats were also likely to educate their children privately rather than send them to the local schools; to use the workplace gym instead of the local leisure centre; to shop and see their friends without needing to mix with anyone living nearby.

How were the churches and other faith groups faring? How were they responding to these changes? It was time to meet them.

Faith communities

Maps, directories, local authority listings and websites gave me the names of faith groups that occupied their own property. But many minority faith groups and independent churches or newer denominations are below the radar: they do not have their own premises. So I made a note of all the signs, A-boards and posters I saw while I walked and cycled around the project area, particularly at weekends. I contacted schools, leisure centres, civic centres, tenants' and residents' halls and church buildings belonging to older denominations which are often hired out for worship. The newer faith communities were often gathered from a wide area, whereas older denominations tended to attract more local residents. The overwhelming majority of faith groups were Christian, with smaller numbers of Buddhist, Muslim and Rastafarian groups with memberships that ranged from 12 to 2,000 people.

Each of the leaders of the 110 faith communities received a questionnaire, and I met or had telephone conversations with 76 of them. Overall, the churchgoing population matched the resident population fairly well in terms of age, ethnicity and socio-economic profile, but there was significant variation between older and newer denominations. Newer churches were younger and very likely to have congregations from mainly black African or black Caribbean communities. Congregations from long-established denominations were more likely to be older and have greater ethnic diversity. There was a mix of people on benefits and in professional or managerial work in almost every faith community.

One of the most significant assets of a faith community in relation to community engagement and regeneration is a building. Those with buildings were not only 'on the map', but were able either to run activities themselves or allow others to do so. There was a great deal of community work taking place, much of it responding to the mental health, financial, housing and educational needs of local people. The most common activity was for the benefit of young people, followed by public meetings, children's education, care for the under-fives, and the elderly. Activities run by others on church premises included the performing arts and work concerning black and minority ethnic issues. Public meetings provided the opportunity for local voices to be heard. Members of faith communities were school governors, were involved in setting up Time Banks, and were on the management committees of local groups, and a few were maintaining good networks and relationships with local councillors and regeneration professionals. Obstacles to further community engagement, including becoming more involved in regeneration activities, were a shortage of time, energy and human resources and a lack of suitable buildings, information and networking. Faith leaders were often fully stretched, but their churches, even those without buildings, often had one particularly valuable asset: the skills necessary to bring different kinds of people together into diverse congregations, negotiating educational, cultural, socio-economic and age boundaries. These skills are used week in and week out and are essential when building healthy, cohesive communities, but the existing demands placed on members of churches and other religious groups meant that they were often unable to share these skills with those already engaged in regeneration.

Churches and minority faith groups were aware of the needs of local people, were engaged in combating poverty, ill health, crime and isolation, and were often speaking out on issues such as the change in rental policy for the Octavia Hill Estate homes. But most of them had little spare energy or enthusiasm for joining another committee, filling in forms, or the networking necessary to become involved in the government-led regeneration taking place.

Opportunities for the Church

It became clear that London South Central was going to change. There was plenty of discussion as to the extent of the change, but the population was set to rise as young professionals moved into the new private-sector flats, changing patterns of residence emerged in social housing, employment opportunities in construction, tourism, the creative industries and in professional and office work opened up, and more support was being offered to those struggling at school or with health difficulties. Along the riverside, luxury housing and commercial premises were being built. Improvements to the Elephant and Castle area and for the large numbers of residents on low incomes living nearby were anticipated but less certain. Changes in society meant that fewer people were dependent on the area where they lived for work, friends, shopping, entertainment or sport, and that more people were living alone. A more fragmented society was a likely result, in which local residents from different housing, income and educational-attainment groups would not necessarily have to meet.

At the same time, government policy was changing, as a result of the Urban White Paper of 2000, in favour of including faith communities in policy-making and decision-making. Neighbourhood Renewal emphasized the involvement in decision-making of those it hoped to benefit. Local Strategic Partnerships, Community Empowerment Networks, Primary Care Trusts, the Metropolitan Police and pan-London bodies such as the Greater London Authority were expected to include churches and other faith groups in their strategic planning.

Churches in London South Central had a history of continuous involvement. Many had buildings, an accessible and inclusive way of working, and worldwide connections. Their members were mostly drawn from the local community. They were concerned with justice, hope, empowerment, and the welfare of all. I recommended that they work in partnership with local authorities, the statutory and voluntary sectors, and regeneration initiatives, to advocate on behalf of those on the margins of society (and facilitate their participation), encourage the kind of regeneration that benefits the whole community, and resist development that could lead to further polarization and fragmentation. Working together across ecclesiastical boundaries would enable them to promote improvements in health, education, housing, employment, and the ability of local people to live life to the full. Bringing their distinctive perspective, local and global, and their particular range of expertise, they would be valuable partners both at a strategic level and in providing accommodation and leadership for pioneering community projects.

Recommendations for the public sector in the report included the need to develop coherent, responsive and less time-consuming ways of engaging with faith communities and encouraging well-informed and active involvement. This is still a challenge: Lambeth Community Empowerment Network currently recommends a three-day course for anyone wanting to join the Local Strategic Partnership.

Since my research, the churches, the boroughs and regeneration partnerships have become better acquainted; multi-faith consultation groups and faith officers have become an accepted part of public life; and the regeneration industry and the Church have tried harder to learn one another's languages. Protests led by local Anglicans continued to the last to save the Octavia Hill Estates (the pioneering affordable housing of the late nineteenth century) from being sold off by the Church Commissioners.

Decision-making in the Church of England is a complicated affair. Whether something happens or not can be the responsibility of a committee, a vicar, a bishop, a synod, or all four. The most likely way in which real and lasting benefits for local people arise from the Church's involvement in regeneration is from discerning, well-focused and sustained engagement. This kind of commitment is not for everyone and partnership working by the Church across ecclesiastical boundaries and with public-sector bodies has not burst on to the regeneration stage of South London. But the Diocese of Southwark has become more alert to the many possibilities, appointing a Regeneration adviser (Tim Scott, see Chapter 7), and more than a few individual parishes have taken up the challenge and pioneered exceptional work, as you will find in the following chapters. Some have joined with other faith and community groups to form South London Citizens, working in partnership with public officials and campaigning for better housing, healthcare and a humane immigration service.

A new project, Faith in Regeneration, was started in London South Central and a development worker appointed. Sonya Brown works with faith organizations from different religious traditions and supports their work with families with the overall aim of reducing child poverty. She also pulls together the well-researched Faith in Regeneration Information Network e-bulletin.

The continued commitment of the Church of England to inner-city people is immensely valuable. An Asset-based Community Development analysis would provide evidence for a vast range of talent, passion, volunteers, global links, credibility, buildings, longevity, green space and expertise. There are now more opportunities than ever not just to run parish-based community development projects in our many buildings, but to bring old wisdom, new energy and a critical edge to local and regional decision-making and to pioneer and model new ways of living creatively and compassionately as communities of hope in our inner cities.

Further reading

Davey, A., *Urban Christianity and Global Order: Theological Resources for an Urban Future*, SPCK, London, 2001.

Edmans, T. and Tarifa, G., *The Regeneration Maze Revisited*, The King's Fund, London, 2001.

Glancey, J., *Bread and Circuses*, Verso, London, 2001.

Hull, John M., *Mission-Shaped Church: A Theological Response*, SCM Press, London, 2006.

Robertson, C., *Regeneration in London South Central*, Southwark and Newington Deanery, London, 2002.

The Scarman Trust, *Asset-Based Community Development*, www.thescarmantrust.org.

4. Thinking Long-term

Keeping Going at the Elephant and Castle

NEIL MCKINNON

Love bears all things, believes all things, hopes all things, endures all things. (1 Corinthians 13.7)

When I mentioned that I was moving to St Matthew's Church at the Elephant and Castle, there were several distinct reactions. The most common was 'That **** pink Shopping Centre?' Another was for the blood to drain from their faces as they repeated 'the Elephant and Castle' in sepulchral tones. My preferred, and indeed the best informed, response was 'You lucky so-and-so, you'll be within walking distance of the Pizzeria Castello!' As I write, this has all changed, but more of that later.

I arrived in the parish in 1995 expecting to work in the 'twelfth most deprived parish in the Diocese of Southwark'. The parish consisted of four large council estates, a large private estate, a church secondary school, a community secondary school and a community primary school, a crown court, the police headquarters, and the pink 1960s Shopping Centre, the first of its kind in Europe. Revised boundaries now mean that the parish runs from the Bricklayers Arms roundabout to the Imperial War Museum. The parish broadens at its centre at the Elephant and Castle itself before narrowing again. This South London real rough diamond parish now also includes South Bank University, the London College of Communication (part of the London University of the Arts), and the Ministry of Sound (some say this is the nation's leading night club). The range of this parish is breathtaking, but somehow it is unlike neighbouring Bermondsey or Walworth or Deptford. It is not a village, one community, but more a series of hamlets.

All roads lead to the Elephant

Throughout history, roads have affected the Elephant. Today, the A2 Dover road and the A23 Brighton road touch the parish tangentially, and the A3 Portsmouth road ploughs through its centre. The roads through the Elephant fragment this community, but of course it was roads that formed the Elephant in the first place.

The Roman Watling Street hugged its way along the lowest dry land above the Thames' tidal plain along the line of the current A2 to the three gravel islands now known as Borough High Street, which determined where London Bridge would be constructed. Gravel islands at St George's Circus and the Elephant and Castle similarly determined where roads could be built. The Roman Stane Street ran through Kennington to the Elephant and St George's Circus to meet Watling Street by St George's Church.

In 1641 John Flaxman established a blacksmith's forge on a site between the roads and a century later this was replaced by an inn called the Elephant and Castle. Various theories exist that explain how the inn was named. Some say it was after the young Infante (princess) de Castile who was to marry an English prince, some say it was named after a mammoth's tooth that had been discovered locally, but those of us who really know admit that nobody knows.

The construction of the New Kent Road and Borough Road in the first half of the eighteenth century secured the pivotal position of the Elephant and Castle. These roads were joined by others serving some of London's new bridges. (Vauxhall, Lambeth, Westminster, Waterloo, Blackfriars, and Southwark Bridges join London Bridge in having a direct road to and through the Elephant and Castle.) By 1906 the Elephant also had two Underground stations.

Southwark 55–54 BC to 1997

Known officially as Holy Trinity with St Matthew, Southwark, the parish is one of only five with 'Southwark' in its title (the others being Southwark Cathedral, St George the Martyr, St Hugh's, and Christ Church). I know of two explanations for the name Southwark. One is that it was the 'South Ward' of the City of London. The other is that since Roman times it had been the southern defence for the City of London, set as it is around the southern side of London Bridge. In the early tenth century it was known as 'Suthringa geworche' (the defensive work of the men of Surrey) and then this was corrupted to mean the southern defences of the City.

The old 'Southwark' would centuries later become the receptacle for all the activities proscribed within the City of London: prostitution; bear-, dog-, and cock-fighting; and the theatre, graced by those luminaries Christopher Marlow and William Shakespeare. The heads of those deemed to be traitors were impaled on the southern end of London Bridge, making it clear to those south of the river that those north of it were in charge.

In the eighteenth century, nearby Walworth and Newington were prosperous suburbs set among market gardens, fields and open marsh land, but a century later the common land had been replaced by Victorian slums.

Charles Dickens, one-time local resident, graphically described the lives of the people living in the slums, the sanctuaries beyond the reach of the law, and the prisons that were such a feature of the district known as Southwark.

Between 1880 and the Blitz at the beginning of World War Two, the Elephant enjoyed its heyday. 'The Piccadilly of South London' boasted many shops and entertainment venues. Perhaps it was the latter's influence that spawned locally born Charlie Chaplin, Tommy Steele, and Michael Caine.

World War Two brought huge destruction to the area, and the planners of the 1960s and 1970s, despite the best of intentions, made it worse. What Hitler's bombers started, they finished. Large-scale demolition enabled the building of the Bricklayers Arms flyover and roundabout (named after a public house that was demolished to make way for it), the Heygate Estate (the Colditz-like building that lines much of the western end of the south side of the New Kent Road), and of course one of London's least liked buildings, the once pink (now red) Elephant and Castle Shopping Centre.

The London Borough of Southwark is the largest landlord in the country. It has many estates that need many millions of pounds spending on them to make them fit for purpose. This applies to a number of the estates at the Elephant.

The Elephant Centre is served by subways that take pedestrians away to areas where, hidden from view, they might become victims of crime. Since the municipal vandalism of the 1960s and 1970s underlined the need for something different, efforts have been made to improve signage, to tile and light the subways, and even to protect them with CCTV cameras. Nothing has had the desired effect. Somehow the area has to become pedestrian-friendly and (even more) car-*unfriendly*. But a problem is that Southwark Council is strapped for cash.

One wise man

Around 1997 a mandarin in the employ of the London Borough of Southwark was looking at the *A to Z Master Atlas of Greater London*. This mandarin had already kick-started the creation of the Tate Modern art gallery, the Millennium Bridge, the Globe Theatre, the regeneration of Bankside, and the renewal of Borough Market, and had seen the Southwark Cathedral extension come into being. This mandarin had another map giving details of all the borough-owned land in the Elephant area. He realized that although the local authority was cash-poor, it was land-rich. He estimated that the London Borough of Southwark owned 90 per cent of the land in the Elephant and Castle area.

Another wise man (or was it woman?)

One day in around 1997 a civil service mandarin in a government office was also looking at the *A to Z Master Atlas of Greater London*. His, or was it her, eye fell on the Elephant and Castle. S/he noticed four things:

1 That the Elephant is the hub of the roads that cross the river between Vauxhall Bridge and London Bridge, that it has two Underground lines (the Northern and the Bakerloo), that it has a British Rail line (Thameslink), and that it has a couple of dozen bus routes – and that any future tram line will go to and through the Elephant.
2 That the Elephant and Castle is actually north of Victoria.
3 That the Elephant is nearer to both the City and the West End of London than Victoria.
4 That the Elephant and Castle should no longer be regarded as South London, but as London South Central reached by the bridges of London South Central.

The scene is set and the remedy is to hand: the Elephant and Castle is a transport hub that is really part of Central London; the council are land-rich; the City of London through its finance houses wants to help with their money and to work collaboratively; and everyone lives happily ever after. Well, not quite. What is to happen to the existing communities within the area? Will the bulldozers just sweep them away?

The Single Regeneration Budget (SRB)

It was June 1997. The post arrived with a thud on the door mat. It included an A5 manila window envelope addressed to 'St Matthew's at the Elephant'. I opened it and saw that it was a general letter inviting any who cared to go to attend a public meeting that would address proposals to regenerate the Elephant and Castle.

This letter did not go to the shredder. It was too important for that – this was our parish. The letter suggested that our views were important and that our contribution would be valued for any proposals that were necessary. I took this at face value. I had seen the borough from a distance for nearly a quarter of a century. For most of those years Southwark seemed to have lagged behind its south-east London partners of Lewisham and Greenwich where I had also worked. But Southwark of late seemed to have turned a corner, and having been the 'also ran' was now beginning to set the South London pace. I now know that this was much to do with the new leader of the council, Jeremy Fraser.

The first consultation meeting was well attended. Over the coming years I would get to know many of the attendees well, and most of them were people of good will. A number of them were people who had good reason to be suspicious of the motives of the council. Time and again those in authority had let them down and they knew from experience that only through standing firm would they survive. The problem was this, though: on this occasion Southwark Council genuinely and seriously wanted their views and their support.

One thing that gave credence to the residents' suspicion was all the haste that was now demanded. Once again meetings were being held in August when many people were on holiday. The real reason for haste in those early days was not immediately clear, but it was this: soon London was to get a mayor who would have sweeping powers for planning, and Southwark Council wanted to get its own plans for the Elephant established before the mayor, whoever that might be, got his or her feet under the table.

While the council busied themselves with outline plans and advertising for potential developers in European journals, the government indicated it might be able to help. It was prepared to pump-prime this £4 billion development in an area equivalent to a quarter of our parish, with £25 million of Single Regeneration Budget (SRB). This money was to be spent largely on schemes in the north of the borough that would encourage capacity building and social inclusion and that would ensure that the existing community would not be swept aside in the regeneration. However, SRB funding had to be bid for, and not all applications were successful. Word on the street had it that the first application was not well received by the Government Office for London. It was later reported that it was only the widespread support for the regeneration from the community that allowed the London Borough of Southwark to have another try: go away and do better next time. No council officer told the community how essential to the bid their support was, and this contributed to the community's wariness.

The next application for SRB funding was successful. There would be an Elephant Links Partnership Board that was to be responsible for the spending of the SRB monies. The council were to be the 'Accountable Body'. The meaning of 'Accountable Body', though, varies:

1 A number of council officers considered that money could be spent only on what they approved.
2 The Education Department officers considered the money to be part of their budget, and thought that the Partnership Board only had to be told what the Education Department had decided.
3 Others took the term 'Accountable' in this context to be what it says – that is, there had to be one party who was responsible for ensuring that public monies were not misused. If we decided to hold a series of workshops in the Bahamas, then the Accountable Body would be there to blow the whistle.

Viewpoints 1 and 2 above tended to prevail.

The Elephant Links Partnership Board

The Elephant Links Partnership Board would have various sub-groups representing residents, local business, the voluntary sector, those interested in the quality of life and the environment, and those who were concerned with training, education and lifelong learning. Later, black and minority ethnic groups had their own representation. Of course, the council and the developer were also to be represented. As the local church, we were concerned that current residents would be pushed out, as seems to have happened elsewhere in the country, not least in Docklands. So we associated ourselves with the group called the Elephant and Castle Residents Regeneration Group. Later the Elephant Links Community Forum was established and again we associated ourselves with it.

The Elephant Links Community Forum

I was elected the first chair of the Elephant Links Community Forum. As such, I negotiated that the Community Forum should have five places on the Partnership Board (out of about 20), which was more than the council (who had four). I negotiated that the quorum for the Elephant Links Partnership Board should be five, of whom at least two must be Community Forum representatives. This I was later to regret, although it seemed prudent at the time. I further negotiated that the Community Forum should have three full-time members of staff (a Director, a Community Development Worker, and an Administrator) and that the Forum should have its own premises and that the SRB should pay its overheads. All this was intended to ensure that the local community could play a positive role in the regeneration, secure in the knowledge that, if needs be and they were threatened with being pushed aside, then they could ultimately resist. I then stood down as chair through exhaustion and the time demands of the role, but continued to work with the Community Forum. This was not always easy, but more of that later.

An early success of the Community Forum concerned social housing (accommodation for rent administered either by the local authority or a housing association). The previous council had wanted 67 per cent (794 units) of the council housing lost by the demolition of the 1,200 units on the Heygate Estate to be replaced with new social housing. The Heygate Estate was central to the regeneration plans. (It was central, and cheaper to pull the Estate down and replace it than to repair it.) We gained an agreement to replace all of the 1,200 units of social housing lost. Subsequent plans have increased this number, but that is with far more housing units being built overall. I understand the current plans to be for 6,600 units of housing (2,200 units of social housing plus 2,200 units for sale, and another 2,200 to be shared equity housing, where residents would pay part-rent and part-mortgage.

The Development Working Group (DWG)

The task of the Elephant Links Partnership Board was expanding beyond simply being responsible for the spending of the SRB money. This was evident in the setting up of another sub-group of the Board. This came to be called the Development Working Group (DWG), and it was asked to indicate its preferred developer. The group worked well and normally consensually. It had representatives from all of the sub-groups of the Board. I was a representative of the Community Forum. Our task was to establish the criteria by which those who had applied to be the developer should be judged: areas included housing, education provision, environment, transport, health and so on. This proved to be a high point in the process. We 'marked' the applications of the would-be developers. Our recommendation for the developer went first to the Community Forum, then to the Partnership Board, and then to the full council. Each of these bodies unanimously adopted the DWG's recommendation to appoint our chosen developer.

The Development Executive Team (DET)

The Development Working Group evolved into the Development Executive Team (DET). It had some members of the DWG, but a number of them, myself included, did not stand. The DET was a kind of triumvirate, representing the council, the developers and the Partnership Board. Its meetings were confidential, and what was considered at the time to be ground-breaking: each grouping had access to its own experts. So the Partnership Board members, as well as the council and the developers, could employ their own specialist lawyers, planners, transport consultants and architects to advise them.

A bridge too far?

Soon, however, other developments would overtake the whole process. The Community Forum started to exercise their effective veto (if they walked out of a meeting of the Partnership Board, the Board would immediately become inquorate). They would withdraw at the slightest provocation, and entire meetings would be taken up agreeing the minutes of the previous meeting. Not infrequently Partnership Board members were subjected to tirades of abuse, and on occasion physical violence, by members of the Community Forum. I have reflected long on how this came to be. The nearest I have got is that some members of the Community Forum had their own agenda that was not related to the overall well-being of the community. People of good will who had previous experience of local authorities abusing their trust colluded with these other voices against the interests of the community.

Community Forum members of the Partnership Board were mandated (they became delegates who were told how they had to vote, rather than representatives who cast their vote according to conscience or the power of reason). Minutes and agenda papers were going out too late from the council officers who serviced the Boards. This allowed those who had time at the last minute to peruse the papers (namely those employed by the Community Forum) to have an advantage over the others. They were able to 'brief' Community Forum Board members in a biased way, which when subsequently checked was found to be partial – incomplete and biased.

The normal development of any new group goes through a process. At the start of the process there will be 'storming', proceeding to 'forming', and then via 'norming' to 'performing'. This simply did not happen with the Elephant Links Community Forum. It was a nightmare scenario.

Jeremy Fraser had stood down as a councillor, and therefore leader, at the election in 1997. Before the next election in 2001, the council's advisers told them that the developers were being too greedy. Simply put, the developers insisted that theirs was a high-risk venture and that they should be allowed to make larger profits as a consequence. The council argued, and I am sure they were right, that there was not a particularly high risk given the location of the Elephant and the council's land assets. There was no agreement, and the developers were sacked. Then almost immediately there was the local election and a new political party came to power via an agreement with the third largest party. I have deliberately avoided naming political parties because at no point in the nine or so years that this process has been in train has the regeneration ever become a party political football. Most wanted the best for the community and the borough.

With the developers gone, the new council administration resented the way that the Partnership Board representatives on the DET, and the erstwhile developers, had seemed to work together against the council. The auditors and the lawyers were called in, and the Partnership Board was stood down along with the Community Forum. A new Partnership Board was set up and I was invited to join it, not as a Community representative but as a 'faith representative'. The new Board had new sub-groups, with names like the Diversity Panel and the Programme Management Panel. Opinion polls and focus groups took over the role that the Partnership Board had played.

Sadly, although the new Board took precautions about who would be acceptable as Community representatives (that they should have a proven track record of being able to work with others, which is not to say that they must always agree), the whole Partnership Board was pushed into a siding. It is a classic case of the baby being thrown out with the bath water, and from then on the Partnership Board was only wheeled out to rubber-stamp decisions regarding spending of SRB monies in amounts of over £100,000, while also being informed that if we did not agree this spending then the London Development Agency would withdraw the funding. Ironically this has mainly concerned two sites that the previous Partnership Board had turned down. Both council-owned, the previous Board considered the sites too far from the Elephant to be an appropriate use of money. The Partnership Board has been given another year to supervise the spending of the remainder of its £25 million (all already allocated).

The Elephant in 2006

Much has happened at the Elephant in the last ten years. It is easy to see that there is already much new physical development. In the part of the parish that lies between Great Dover Street, the New Kent Road and Newington Causeway (the Harper Road triangle), the population has doubled. There are four new gated communities that seem to be made up largely of solicitors, accountants and company directors. There are many new developments in train, but hardly a brick has been laid in the main Elephant regeneration plan. So far there is one smallish block of housing in nearby Wansey Street. The main development has hardly begun, but the SRB money was meant to have been used by March 2006. We have spent some money on making features of our railway bridges and illuminating buildings and trees. There is certainly a feelgood factor to this.

Hoardings have started to go up around buildings that are to be demolished prior to development. The Pizzeria Castello has closed. Soon the 2 kilometres of subways that connect the centre of the Elephant will be filled in and replaced by surface crossings, and the southern roundabout will be removed and the nearby open space will be landscaped. As the residents currently living on the Heygate are decanted into the smaller blocks as they are built, the Heygate Estate will be demolished in stages, clearing the way for the major part of the regeneration of the Elephant. It will be one of the largest regeneration projects ever seen in Europe.

When the regeneration is complete it will provide 6,600 new homes, a straightened and pedestrianized Walworth Road lined with shops, a better-integrated public transport network, a market place, restaurants, cafés, pubs, cinemas, art galleries and leisure centres; and a public square on the northern roundabout will connect with the new line of Walworth Road: all the facilities one would expect in a Central London community. The arches that carry the railway will be opened to improve access, and to allow the Elephant to become a real community and a true village. Word has it that the Elephant will be seen by everyone as the *real* centre of Southwark and that a new town hall containing all council departments will be built here.

The Elephant and Castle Trust

A new charitable body has been established as the Elephant and Castle Trust. It is a Development Trust that will seek to attract money from a wide variety of sources, both to mitigate the effect of, and to build on, the challenges of the regeneration. It is modelled on the well-established Paddington Trust. It has as trustees a number of the great and the good, including the vice-chancellor of South Bank University, the local MP, and the leader of Southwark Council. Others of us are make-weights. This time I am not there as a member of our community, or as a 'faith representative', but as myself. This I regret.

In conclusion

Would I do it again? Yes, I would. I am an Anglican, and St Matthew's at the Elephant is Anglican. I have lived and/or worked in what we now call Urban Priority Areas for most of my life, and for the majority of my ordained ministry I have worked alongside the community. It hasn't always been easy. I had not expected all this to happen at the Elephant, but the letter had arrived and we couldn't ignore it.

One day some years ago an incumbent of a successful Central London church came to my door. Looking up at the surrounding tower blocks, he said, 'I wouldn't have a clue about how to minister around here.' Generally speaking, my experience of inner-city churches is that they serve their communities and the wider Church well. We start where people are: we look to the Incarnation for that. Everybody in the land can look to their parish church for baptism, marriage and burial. I would argue that they should be able to look to us during the intervening parts of their lives, both as individuals and as a community.

I would not argue that this is an exclusively Anglican insight (not all Anglicans would see it this way, and many clergy and churches of other denominations would). However, having worked in an ecumenical team, my experience is that Anglicans are more likely to see it this way, and other denominations less likely. It is one reason why I believe passionately in the parochial system: it provides a focus for our mission, and that includes social action. Some of those who know me are surprised to discover that I believe firmly in the Established Church. I suspect that the Church of England would benefit from disestablishment, but I suspect that our society would be impoverished by it. This follows from a firm belief in the Incarnation, that the sacred is to be found within the secular.

We have a large Muslim community in the parish. Many viewed St Matthew's with suspicion before the regeneration process, and some still do. However, because many of the Partnership Board meetings, Community Forum meetings and many workshops have been held here in St Matthew's, many Muslims have started to use our buildings. We now have two exclusively Muslim women's groups. Muslims have been thrilled to be able to say their prayers in our building during the week, and one group even asked if they could hold their regular Friday Prayers here. I doubt that would have happened without the regeneration process. Again, following what we now call 9/11, 7/7 and the Iraq War, we have opened our chapel during the week to members of the public for prayer or meditation. Again, I think this said something, not least because a number of Muslims have been assaulted locally during these periods.

Another question is the involvement of lay people from the congregation. Areas like the Elephant normally have a high turnover within the community, and with the regeneration this has greatly increased. All of the people from the congregation who were involved in the process have, ironically, moved on. This also applies to the other clergy from local churches.

A question that should be asked is this: if you have a loyalty to people who live in social housing, where is your loyalty to be found when half or perhaps more of the community is in owner-occupied or shared equity housing? Of course we must respond to them. Indeed, perhaps the Church alone can offer a home to the whole community, artisans and accountants. But the biblical imperative must always be to stand beside the marginalized and oppressed.

One last thought is that the Almighty has a sense of humour. I suspect that I have long enjoyed an inverted snobbery about working in deprived areas. When I arrived this was the twelfth poorest parish in the Diocese of Southwark. When I take my leave of this parish, it may well be the twelfth richest in the Diocese. I can sense the Divine smile looking down and saying that it is not so much where you work, only that you are faithful.

Further reading

Chanan, G. and West, A. with Garratt, C. and Humm, J., *Regeneration and Sustainable Communities*, Community Development Foundation, London, 1999.

Commission on Urban Life and Faith, *Faithful Cities: A Call for Celebration, Vision and Justice*, Church House Publishing/Methodist Publishing House, London, 2006.

Department of the Environment, *Effective Partnerships*, Department of the Environment, London, 1997.

Department of the Environment, *SRB Challenge Fund: Handbook of Good Practice in Management Systems*, Department of the Environment, London, 1997.

ECOTEC Research & Consulting Limited, *Elephant Links SRB Partnership Audit Report*, ECOTEC Research & Consulting Limited, Birmingham, 2003.

Local Government Management Board, *Creating Community Visions*, Local Government Management Board, London, 1996.

MCA Regeneration, *Interim Evaluation of the Elephant Links Community Forum*, MCA Regeneration, London, 2002.

Regeneration & Transport Scrutiny Sub-committee of the London Borough of Southwark, *Public Consultation in Relation to the Elephant & Castle Regeneration Project: Final Report*, Southwark Borough Council, London, June 2004.

Reilly, L., *Southwark: An Illustrated History*, London Borough of Southwark, London, 1998.

Urban Task Force chaired by Lord Rogers of Riverside, *Towards an Urban Renaissance*, E. & F. N. Spon (Taylor & Francis Group plc), London, 1999.

www.elephantandcastle.org.uk

5. In the Middle of It

Co-operation and Resistance on the Ferrier Estate

NICK RUSSELL AND CHARLIE INGRAM

Let us then pursue what makes for peace and for mutual edification. (Romans 14.19)

The Ferrier Estate lies between Kidbrooke and Eltham in the London Borough of Greenwich. Some 5,000 people live there. There are 1,910 local authority homes, about 160 of which have been bought under the 'right-to-buy' legislation and the rest of which are rented. The estate also contains two primary schools and has a secondary school on its doorstep. Although very deprived, it is an exemplary multi-cultural community, and about 60 per cent of the residents are black and minority ethnic, many of whom are refugees. The estate is to be replaced by a housing association estate of 4,398 homes, only 1,350 of which will be affordable rented homes, though 550 will be shared equity/keyworker dwellings. The rest of the properties will be private sales.

We work together on the estate: Nick as a Church Army community evangelist and church planter, and Charlie as a Baptist minister (yes, that's right) of the Church of England's Church of the Holy Spirit: a shopfront church on the estate. We work together, but we have rather different roles, as the two sections of this chapter will show.

Resistance

Nick Russell

Government money for the Ferrier's regeneration was obtained on the basis of bettering the lives of the community. FRAG, the Ferrier Residents' Action Group, was set up under government consultation requirements originally as the FSG (Ferrier Steering Group) as a residents' group, but became a strong voice of protest and campaigning as residents' interests were in reality sacrificed. After the (ongoing) compulsory displacement ('decant') of nearly a third of the households, there is currently no new build and will not be for some time to come. The council have persistently rejected the idea of build first, decant second.

I became involved in FRAG shortly after coming to live on the estate as a Church Army community evangelist and church planter, became vice-chair, and ended up as chair by default when a previous chair resigned. I can only say that all of us on the FRAG committee started out with a real hope of working with Greenwich Council to make the regeneration into something all could be proud of, but we were quickly disillusioned and became an embattled group in an unwanted community, as the following story (which does not detail all of the abuses) recounts.

The story of sacrificing a community to government housing targets and policies began in the autumn of 1999 with a phone call to the embryonic FSG from the council's South Greenwich Regeneration Agency (SGRA). It gave us a mere 24 hours' notice of a public meeting on the Ferrier Estate. Hastily, we plastered the Estate with posters, and we were delighted with the result. A packed school hall heard the council announcing that it had chosen the option of comprehensive demolition and redevelopment rather than the options of refurbishment or of a mix of the two.

Many anxious voices were raised. What would happen to existing residents? Could they develop without moving people away? Would the community be dispersed? Would the community benefit? Unsubstantiated bland assurances were given. (Reports commissioned by the SGRA suggested that the scheme at the time was merely a plan to capitalize on the value of land near to Blackheath to interest private developers.) This tactic became usual over the next few years, and the reality only became apparent after all the necessary consultations and consents had been achieved. People that night were unconvinced. No opportunity to vote was offered, and the council attempted to curtail protests and control the meeting.

A few nights later, as the SGRA presented their case for funding from central government grants, they gave assurances that residents supported the demolition option. We were stunned and horrified by the sheer dishonesty of this statement, although it was later to pale into insignificance. The Bishop of Woolwich at the time, Colin Buchanan, was with us at that meeting as we sat in the tiny area (about six seats) for the public. More than once the sight of his purple shirt at meetings disconcerted the council. We took our protests to the public gallery in the Town Hall at the next meeting of the full council, where I demanded a 'right to return' – that is, for residents to be able to move into the new homes in the redevelopment (couched in question form as required). Councillors looked stunned. They had imagined that this was all about new homes for Ferrier residents, and must have been surprised that no right to return to the new homes had been given. Chris Roberts, the leader of the council, made an angry reply, ignoring the question. We had been alarmed by the background reports commissioned by the council, talking about the blight on land values of the Ferrier Estate. Worse, there was a report called *Kidbrooke Development Area* by a Greenwich Council officer which explicitly said that while comprehensive redevelopment would break up the Ferrier community, the removal of 'negative' networks would benefit security in the wider south Greenwich area. (This ignored the fact that Ferrier crime rates were lower than in surrounding estates.)

In a move that looked disingenuous to us, Greenwich councillors at the meeting were assured that a 'yes' decision only meant an exploration of the comprehensive demolition and redevelopment option, not a decision to carry it out. The large Labour majority fell into line, as usual.

There then followed a lull in tension as masterplanners came on board. They were a nice group of people who wanted to know exactly what we would like to see in the redeveloped area. Confidence began to rise, and assurances were given that a minimal amount of residents would have to move, for just a short time, and that they would be allowed to return to the new homes. We did not receive a legal right to return, but an assurance from a councillor that 'all those who wished to remain living in the area would be able to do so as a result of the redevelopment'.

The Masterplan was eventually published, a glossy document with too little detail and no legal guarantees. As the residents' group, we were asked to endorse it. We held a public meeting to which about 300 people came, packing out the Community Hall. Our residents' independent adviser presented the Masterplan and FRAG conducted a secret ballot. The ballot gave people the option of a straightforward endorsement, a straightforward rejection, an endorsement provided there was a right to return and a ballot on a legally binding residents' charter (setting out the details of the redevelopment), and a 'don't know'. Some 90 per cent of the vote was for an endorsement with the proviso of a ballot on a legally binding residents' charter and a right to return. We made this position clear at the next meeting with the council, to their disgust. Their press office issued a typically distorted release, saying simply that 90 per cent of Ferrier residents supported the Masterplan.

Over a period of months, with the help of 'First Call', our Residents' Independent Adviser, paid for under government guidelines by the council, we developed a Residents' Charter. (The Adviser was subsequently axed by the council.) The Charter set out what was required to create an estate suitable for major groups such as the large number of lone parents and the young people who needed facilities to help prevent them drifting into vandalism and crime. At each stage of its development we held public meetings to receive comments and then to obtain general endorsement from the Estate in general. The council refused to allow this document a role in the regeneration process. To their annoyance, I later e-mailed it to prospective developers as they prepared their bids.

The council had to obtain resident approval of the Masterplan. This they did by distributing a glossy shortened version of the already scantily detailed document. Few people responded, but of those who did a high percentage endorsed the plan. This came as no surprise. It seemed to be a simple promise along the lines of 'new homes for old'. The devil, as we later found out, was in the detail. The Deputy Prime Minister's office required a statutory consultation. This came in the form of a turgid document which also left out important details. Simultaneously, we obtained about 400 signatures on letters objecting to the lack of guarantees for residents. There was no agreed Residents' Charter and no right to return. We presented these at the Office of the Deputy Prime Minister and hoped for an investigation. Instead we got a reply from a civil servant that seemed as if he had cut and pasted from a Greenwich Council propaganda document. No independent attempt was made to ascertain the facts. The council was being backed, it seemed, by the New Labour government.

The next disaster was the council's 'Ferrier Rehousing Strategy'. Homeloss compensation ('crying money' for the inconvenience and disruption) was fixed by central government, but Disturbance Payments (to cover the actual costs of moving) were set by the council. We were dismayed by their intentions. Ferrier homes are much larger than almost any other affordable homes in the borough, and of a practically unique design. Many would have to discard and replace furniture too large to fit into replacement homes. This furniture had been saved for and bought by people on low incomes, but there was to be no compensation for this. There would be compensation for carpets and curtains that would not fit replacement homes, but this was set at half their secondhand value, a ridiculous concept. How could they be replaced by people on low incomes or on benefits? Contrary to previous bland assurances, removals would be paid one way only. Who would be able to pay out to return? In their strategy, the council stated it was prepared to make two offers of alternative council accommodation to secure tenants, and would then take legal action. However, these offers are made one at a time, and people feel afraid that the second might be worse, and often take the first, fearing court action. Letters going to tenants offering (more expensive) housing association accommodation imply that failure to accept such offers may prejudice further offers.

Moreover, it fast became apparent that building of affordable homes for rent would proceed at roughly one-third of the pace of homes for sale. With the people remaining on the estate being given the top priority for these affordable homes, those moving away had little chance for years to come. We calculated that at least half of the residents would have been dispersed before there was an opportunity to move into the new homes. The decant, at a rate of about five households per week, began in 2004, but there will be no new homes to move into until 2009 at the earliest, and even then only a proportion will be affordable homes for rent. With removals paid only one way, the redevelopment is clearly only going to benefit a tiny minority of the existing community, if any at all.

Just as decanting started, a number of shop premises on the estate had their rents increased, including the local supermarket. Over many months the council prevaricated and gave excuses over negotiations on these rents. At the time of writing, they are encouraging the shopkeepers to sell out at the earliest opportunity, making life very difficult for the elderly and lone parents on the estate, and increasing the incentive to accept any kind of move at the earliest opportunity. The supermarket has already given up and closed.

Meanwhile homeowners were offered such low purchase prices (e.g. £90,000 for a four-bedroom house with front and back gardens!) that acceptance would be tantamount to making themselves homeless. They are determined to fight to the end, and to object to and delay a Compulsory Purchase Order. (This can only happen when it can be demonstrated that the scheme is going ahead, and at the time of going to press this is still not certain.) Many are left isolated in deserted decanted areas. One homeowner has, at the time of writing, been left entirely isolated in a 12-storey block surrounded by metal sheeting on her landing which leaves it dark and menacing. She was burgled and also suffered flood damage from a leak in an unoccupied flat. The council's proposed solution? An introductory tenancy (i.e. with no right to compensation until 12 months have elapsed) in her own flat, on condition that she agrees to the council's asking price (around £60,000). Her story appeared in the *South*

London Press with the headline 'This place is like a prison'. She asked to be allocated a flat in a less isolated position temporarily, but this was said by the council to be a disincentive for her to sell.

The developer/housing association partnership for this £0.75 billion deal was selected, without notice in council agendas, by two councillors sitting on 23 December 2005, ignoring preferences expressed by the Ferrier community and people from surrounding neighbourhoods.

Written questions to the full council were, in many cases, receiving misleading written answers. I realized that in most instances the questions were probably not understood by councillors, and possibly were not even being read. However, we knew that there was some disquiet over the regeneration. In the run-up to local elections in May 2006, I organized a tactic of asking the important questions as supplementaries, which we were able to ask out loud in the council chamber. On one of these occasions my supplementary was 'The Council's report, *The Kidbrooke Development Area*, talks about the benefit of dispersing residents of the Ferrier. Is it the Council's intention to disperse the Ferrier community?' It was the only time that I saw every face in the Labour group turn towards the public gallery. Later, we learned that there would be an increase in the numbers of homes built in the first phase, which may have been a victory for our efforts.

The council's 'lettable standard' was exposed for the sham it is when a local newspaper carried a shocking article on a replacement home (in a later decant phase on the Ferrier) declared by a council manager to be at a lettable standard. Tim, a council employee who had to take early retirement on health grounds, spent a great deal of his own money redecorating this home. It is now possible that he will have to move again because of the developer's plans. He says, 'I can't face going through it all again. I expected to be here for a good few years. I'm stressed out. My wife is stressed out.' The decant was planned and begun before a developer was even selected, and obviously before the developers' plans were known. Homeloss payments are being used to pay for redecorating and refurbishing replacement homes, and to replace furniture that won't fit. (Tim's Homeloss payment was withdrawn two days before Christmas 2005 because he was deemed to have moved 'voluntarily' within the estate.) The decant is leaving people isolated and surrounded with empty homes which, in many cases, become occupied by rats and other vermin.

In spite of the council's promise to allow people who depended on one another to remain close together, sick relatives have been separated from their carers, and lone parents have had to give up work because they are now separated from friends and family who supplied after-school childcare.

Why should a community evangelist get involved in a local campaign? 'You trample on the poor' (Amos 5.11) is the frequent reproof by prophets against the powerful and rich in Israel, and remains true today as governments see their votes coming from the majority middle class. Our Christian mission on the estate works on the principle of 'Blessing, Belonging' before 'Believing, Behaving' – that is, on signs of God's love in practical and believable forms and for a community that finds it difficult to believe in a loving God amid long-term deprivation and injustice.

The decant continues, while new build is delayed. Many feel that their basic human rights are being abused and that the council has turned their home environment into a desolate, forbidding and frightening place, under a scheme whose planning was funded by central government ostensibly to benefit the existing community. We continue to try to persuade officials in various quarters to change the scheme so that local people benefit, rather than pay the price for benefiting others who are better off than themselves – a pattern often seen in the history of redevelopments. 'They covet fields, and seize them; houses, and take them away; they oppress householder and house, people and their inheritance' (Micah 2.2).

Co-operation

Charlie Ingram

The regeneration of the Ferrier Estate is happening. We are definitely 'in the middle of it' and, arguably, it needs to happen. Over the years neglect has made this a place where people with choice don't choose to live. It is a mixed community that includes many disempowered people, whose circumstances are such that they find themselves marginalized and disadvantaged by society, whether for financial reasons (through low wages or unemployment) or as a result of migration, poor mental health, or addictions. Many have lived here for a long time. Some moved into the flats in the early 1970s when they were new and the estate hailed the promise of a modern new future; others (although a minority) have bought their homes, exercised their right-to-buy, and expected to live out their days in their own home.

The estate has a strong identity. It is architecturally distinct from the surrounding area, the high-rise grey concrete blocks giving it an imposing feel; but with that comes a strong sense of local identity.

Ferrier residents seem to support one another in a way that those in neighbouring communities once used to. Families in nearby Blackheath, with more disposable income, buy in the services they need. Here, on the estate, there is still a reliance on extended family, friends and the community. The shared experience of living here, and being the subject of others' preconceptions and prejudices, has built strong bonds.

This estate belongs to them – it is their home and it is their community, not simply a potential extension to the wealthier community of Blackheath. Any regeneration should surely be for their benefit and not simply for the gentrification of the area? For current residents to benefit, the regeneration needs be delivered with the minimum of disruption. Residents need to be involved – not only consulted with, but also listened to. What is so disappointing, as Nick's story illustrates so well, is that this is not happening. Local people are being ignored, and up to 50 per cent will be moved out to make way for the bulldozers. The council says that 'any resident who wishes to remain living in the area will be able to do so as a result of the scheme', though in practice it will be five to ten years before those being moved out now can exercise this right. Most will have settled away from the area during that time and I doubt that many will choose to return.

If the Church is to live out Jesus' manifesto of being 'good news to the poor', then we must challenge injustice. We must have a voice calling those responsible to account. We cannot be afraid to stand with the community and we must, if necessary, resist. Jesus wasn't afraid to challenge injustice and was often seen by the leaders of his day as a troublemaker. Preaching peace and love doesn't get you crucified. Jesus empowered the poor, sided with the marginalized, befriended the socially excluded, and became a thorn in the side of the powerful. Such behaviour will earn you the attention of the authorities and can get you killed. We cannot sit back and watch as the poor and the disempowered are moved out of this community to make way for others, simply because the land they are living on has increased in value exponentially and made its 'regeneration' commercially profitable. We should rightly be involved in the local residents' action group, helping to empower people, informing them of their rights, supporting them, standing with them, and fighting with them.

Yet we must also realize that this stance of resistance has a cost. After years of campaigning for residents' rights, FRAG find themselves being marginalized by those in control of the regeneration and sidelined as opponents of progress. In reality this is not the case because fighting for residents' rights within the scheme is different from opposing it entirely. Yet it may be that giving residents their rights, compensating them adequately, reducing the number of homes for sale so that all the current residents can live in the new social housing, is simply too expensive. It could make the scheme so unattractive to a developer with one eye on their share value that they might pull out altogether. In order for the scheme to go ahead the council appear to need the unquestioning co-operation of the existing community. Any group empowering them to do otherwise are seen as troublemakers who need removing, disempowering, discrediting, or at least containing, so that they can do as little damage as possible to the council's vision of the future.

With this in mind, how closely should the Church align itself with FRAG and their position? If the Church is also seen as part of the resistance, we too will be marginalized and eventually ignored as the new community is built around us. The impact on the Church of our post-Christian culture is well documented elsewhere, but, put simply, gone are the days when the Church enjoyed a default position of authority within a community. In this new post-Christian secular world we need to earn our place and argue for the value of our contribution alongside other faith groups and voluntary organizations. Not everyone sees this as a bad thing, and neither do I. Unless we can find a more conciliatory voice, one that can engage more constructively with the regeneration here in Kidbrooke, we risk being left out altogether. The estate will be flattened and rebuilt, and an opportunity for the Church to be involved in the future here would have been missed and that would be a tragedy.

In addition, we have no building of our own with which to negotiate. Holy Spirit Church is a church plant that serves the Ferrier Estate from a leased shop unit on the estate. It seems to me that the majority of those churches that have benefited from regeneration schemes, including a number in this book, have done so because of the location of their building. It might be that the church building is a piece of protected heritage architecture so prominent within the regeneration scheme that the developer needs to build around it and design a scheme to enhance it. Or if the building is of no particular historical interest, it could be that regeneration is best served by its demolition – and with it the provision of a new space for the church as compensation. Either way it is the ownership of a property within the area that is a catalyst for the churches' involvement. We don't own a building at Holy Spirit Church: all we have is a lease and a moral argument. Our building is well used, but in the hard-nosed world of business we need to find some way to put tangible value on the church and our contribution to the estate. Otherwise, when our lease is up in October 2007, the council may simply refuse to renew it and ask us to leave.

Not that having our own space is a prerequisite of our continued existence on the estate. Part of me thinks that the loss of our building could be the creative impetus we need. However, it seems right that we should first be involved with the regeneration discussions, trying to win the provision of a new church for the benefit of the future community, before considering second and third options.

I arrived as minister of Holy Spirit Church in the summer of 2004. Nick was doing a fantastic job as chair of FRAG and initially I thought about publicly joining their campaign. However, strategically, I felt we needed a different approach.

In our dealings with Greenwich Council we needed both a co-operative approach and a critical approach, yet in reality working closely together. With this in mind I have attempted to develop a positive relationship with members of the council. Were Nick not here, doing what he's doing, I would not, in good conscience, be free to take the more conciliatory position.

We need to find a way to keep the Church 'in' the Kidbrooke vision, bringing the skills and enthusiasm we have to the table. We need to find a way to work with the council to realize the best for the area, believing that God has placed us here, both now and for the future. Strategically we hope that this differentiation of our roles as good cop and bad cop is allowing this to happen.

£239,000 a year, freely given to the Ferrier community by Christians

That got their attention! This was our headline on a letter to the council in May 2005 and it seemed to work. We had calculated a financial value of the current provision being given to the Ferrier Community by Ferrier Focus (a strategic partnership between Holy Spirit Church, St James, Kidbrooke, Eltham Green Christian Centre, and Greenwich Youth for Christ). Christians from different denominations have been serving the Ferrier community since it was built. We needed the council to see and to acknowledge the contribution that the Church is making to this community. Put in regeneration language, we tried to put a financial value on the social capital or community profit we bring. Let us not be afraid to recognize our many strengths. The Church has much to offer to a regeneration scheme of this nature, for in the main we 'do community' well. At the root of our faith we have a God who is Trinity: Father, Son and Holy Spirit, love in community. All the orthodox traditions from Greek Orthodox to the Free Churches express the desire to reflect this understanding in our meeting and being together.

First, we gather people together, often from diverse backgrounds. At Holy Spirit Church, we have Nigerians, Ghanaians, Sierra Leoneans and West Indians as well as both black and white British. With church attendance in London now black majority, many councils and government bodies are seeing the churches as a way to communicate with the black community. This was well illustrated at a recent stakeholder meeting when a representative from a specialist ethnic minority housing association asked me if we had good contacts with the other faith/ethnic communities. We are seen as a potential way to access the black African community that makes up much of the churchgoing population of the estate.

Second, we come together voluntarily. With the possible exception of the minister, no one is paid to come to church. We can gather a community together, organize them, often feed them, and resource our meetings with all that is necessary, from stewards to PA systems – all voluntarily. This is a skill we have that we need to recognize.

Third, we are deeply involved in our communities. We are here, on the ground, striving to incarnate the gospel, while many (if not all) of the councillors and officers are not a part of the community. They work remotely, visiting the estate as little as possible. We have been here since the estate was built, we are here now, and our desire is to be here in the future. We are not planning on going anywhere.

Fourth, we are serving the community, and people know that we care. We deliver everything from youthwork to care for the elderly. We are good at identifying and tackling local needs, as we see them being expressed week in, week out. Once a need is identified, we can mobilize and motivate people to serve their community. This activism is a real strength and is a resource of tangible value to the council and its developer as they seek to regenerate the area.

Finally, and perhaps more specific to the Ferrier Estate, we can speak on behalf of the churches. Mission on the Ferrier is thoroughly ecumenical and built on strong relationships between local churches. Under the banner of Ferrier Focus, Christians have come together in partnership and mission, resourcing work that none of us would have managed on our own. Anglicans, Baptists, Free Evangelicals and a local Christian charity all work together to serve the community. We have a stronger voice when we speak together.

With all this in mind, and armed with a well-drafted paper outlining our desire to partner with the council, we approached the lead councillor for regeneration and the Kidbrooke project team for a meeting. They responded positively and three of us from Ferrier Focus made our way to the town hall for a meeting.

No sooner had we shaken hands and sat down around the table

than the lead councillor for regeneration asked me: 'What's your relationship with Nick Russell?'

Thus there was no enquiry as to the purpose of our meeting – instead a question designed quickly and simply to assess our position and set the tone for the rest of the meeting. In response I explained that we work closely with Nick and support the work of FRAG, but that today we were meeting to discuss a different issue, namely, how the Church could work with the council to help deliver the potential Kidbrooke vision. We wanted to communicate and focus on some of the strengths of the Church on the Ferrier Estate and on the good things we have to offer the regeneration scheme. From then on the meeting changed tone, and hopefully good seeds were planted for the future.

Since then Nick and I have stuck to our separate roles and agendas. At stakeholder meetings, FRAG asks questions of justice, while I try to stick to issues of partnership and how the Church can work constructively with the council. It is not yet clear whether this strategy is working, and the council officers are still suspicious. This was clearly illustrated at a recent stakeholder meeting when the lead officer answered FRAG's questions while obviously looking for my reactions.

Strategically, I continue to try to strengthen the churches' position within the stakeholder group which should become the developer's primary vehicle for negotiating the future community provision. Nearly a year ago, at the council's request, I convened a meeting of community groups interested in making use of an empty community building on the estate. In one evening we had representatives from 15 local community groups, from all faiths and none and from several different continents, with interpreters, discussing how we could share this facility and make it available, once again, for the community to use (something I don't think the council thought possible). Unfortunately, at the time of writing, the premises are still not open and several community groups, with funding, are without a space to use, but we are assured it will be on the developer's agenda once they are signed up, a process that seems to be taking for ever. Currently, we are waiting for the council and their preferred developer to sign the comprehensive development agreement before we can proceed with the next stage of talking with the developer directly. During this time the council have been keen to control all communication with the developer in order to limit external influences on their negotiations. We are all hoping that the subsequent dialogue with the developer will prove more fruitful for the community.

It can be hard keeping positive in the face of such bureaucracy and procrastination. As I write, the negotiations with the developer are in their twelfth month and should have been completed in three. But we remain hopeful and committed to the long haul.

As we wait, it is worth remembering that the council officers are human too. In our conversations and negotiations I am reminded of Jesus calling to Zacchaeus, the tax collector, undoubtedly an unpopular man in the area, 'I must stay at your house today' (Luke 19.5). The council officers may be seen locally by many as the enemy because of their treatment of local residents, but they are people in need of God's love too, with families and mortgages, responsibilities and insecurities. It can't be easy managing the many demands of a £0.75 billion redevelopment. Maybe there is even the opportunity of ministry to them? Building positive relationships with the council-lors and officers could be an opportunity. I don't always have to agree with them to develop a relationship of mutual respect, do I?

In the meantime the decant rolls on and empty properties are a magnet for squatters, arson and vandalism. The estate has a despon-dent feeling of resignation about it. It is, therefore, *so* important that the church is here being light and blessing to this community, assuring those who remain of their worth before God, when they are being sent so many messages to the contrary.

'Good cop, bad cop' or 'resistance and co-operation': is this a successful strategy? If you can think of a better one, then let us know. Otherwise, we'll find out in about ten years' time.

Further reading

Eastman, M. and Latham, S. (eds), *The Urban Church: A Practitioner's Resource Book*, SPCK, London, 2004.
Murray, S., *Church after Christendom*, Paternoster, Carlisle, 2005.

6. Now It's Done

The North Peckham Estate after the Makeover

JIM JELLEY

[Christ] himself is before all things, and in him all things hold together. (Colossians 1.17)

My footsteps echoed on the iron bridge that joined the vicarage to Farnborough Way, the main walkway of the North Peckham Estate. It was dark and cold and I had to visit a family who lived at the other end. It was a long walk, and felt longer if you were a bit apprehensive and it was dark. Footsteps coming up behind you always felt threatening. Despite having lived and worked in two tough South London parishes, in Stockwell and the Old Kent Road, walking down Farnborough Way at night I felt more exposed and vulnerable than ever before. It was a lonely walk and I didn't hang about. At intervals there were walkways branching off to right and left, and in between were the gloomy entrances to the maisonettes above and below the walkway, three doors up a short stairway, and three doors down a short stairway. It wasn't easy to see the door numbers, so I had to go up – or maybe down – to see if I was in the right place. After the visit it was the long walk back. My footsteps echoed on the iron bridge again. Home at last! I opened the front door with a certain relief.

In the two years or so that I experienced Farnborough Way, a 'muggers' paradise', I was never mugged, or saw a mugging or any other crime taking place, but I always felt a bit apprehensive walking down there, especially at night. Perhaps it was its design that made it seem threatening, or maybe it was more the fearsome reputation of North Peckham that played on my mind. By the time I arrived as parish priest of St Luke's Church in 1996, the decision to regenerate the area had been taken.

The regeneration of North Peckham, which comprised five estates (Camden, Gloucester Grove, Sumner, Willington, and North

Peckham) began in 1994, and it is still going on, so it's not all over yet. Anyone coming back to visit North Peckham couldn't possibly say 'It hasn't changed a bit'. Change, at least in the physical environment, has been massive. The regeneration programme was the biggest in Europe. Given the huge cost of the programme and the inevitable disruption to local people's lives, and the fact that three of the estates, Camden, Gloucester Grove and North Peckham, were only built 30–35 years ago, why was it thought necessary to undertake the regeneration of North Peckham on such a scale?

The refurbishment of the Willington Estate had already begun, and so the regeneration programme centred on the other four estates. Sumner Estate was made up of pre- and post-war blocks of flats, 1930s and 1950s, but the Camden, Gloucester Grove and North Peckham Estates were only built in the late 1960s and early 1970s. These three estates were built according to a vision that was popular at the time. This vision was all concrete and asphalt and paving, communal heating and gardens, underground car-parking and small fenced-in games areas, and blocks of flats and maisonettes with long, internal corridors (Gloucester Grove) or walkways above ground connecting up the blocks (North Peckham) or long external communal balconies (Camden). All had a high density of population with one landlord, the local authority (Southwark Borough Council).

Examples of this vision can still be seen all across London. These three estates, like all similar ones, looked hard and forbidding places whose very design increased social stress and allowed crime to flourish. By the 1980s the North Peckham Estate, as the five estates became collectively known, had a soaring crime rate, especially for burglary and street robbery. In 1993–4 there were 2,100 reported residential burglaries.[1] Not surprisingly, the fear of crime soared too. 'It was scary,' said Victoria, who came to live on the North Peckham Estate in the early 1990s. She recalled seeing handbags discarded by robbers on the stairwells and walkways, so she never carried one around on the estate.

As well as a soaring crime rate and a consequent increase in the fear of crime and of feeling unsafe, there was high unemployment and low educational achievement. By the 1980s the North Peckham Estate had become a byword for crime and deprivation and a place to be avoided; a place where even postal deliveries were suspended for a time; a place where you didn't open your front door at night; a place where you didn't go out after dark; a place where you feared being burgled; a place where the walkways and stairwells smelt of urine, and rubbish was strewn around; and a place of graffiti-covered walls. North Peckham's reputation went before it, in Southwark and beyond.

For many residents of the North Peckham Estate it was a depressing and stressful place to live, and it was a constant battle to survive. For some residents, while acknowledging the difficulties, it was a more positive experience. 'Everyone knew each other on their landing and looked out for each other. It was exciting – all the arguments and the gossip' (Blossom B: Camden Estate resident for 24 years). 'I enjoyed it, especially the launderette, where you met up with people and gossiped. I made friends and we're still in contact' (Blossom J: North Peckham resident for 25 years). There was friendship and neighbourliness on the five estates and good things happened through the Pitt Street Settlement, the Adventure Playground, the Saturday School in the Tenants hall, and the North Peckham Advice Shop.

If the socio-economic factors pointed strongly to a need for regeneration, the fearsome reputation of the North Peckham Estate ensured that it wasn't just refurbishment and improvement that was required, but almost complete destruction of the old vision for communal living. A new vision was needed, and the go-ahead for regeneration came in 1994.

A Master Plan was drawn up and work began in April 1995. The Master Plan allowed for some blocks of flats on the Gloucester Grove and North Peckham Estates to be refurbished and improved by cutting long walkways into two and installing entryphones. The rest were to be bulldozed and replaced with streets with terraced housing and gardens, with very small blocks of flats on the corners of some streets and with a lower density of population. Not exactly a new vision, but one that took account of the need for personal space. It was a design that would not only be more attractive, but would reduce social stress and opportunities for crime – especially burglary and street robbery. An important aspect of the regeneration programme was to have mixed-housing tenure. Before, it was almost solidly local authority-owned. The Master Plan for the five estates proposed the following:

Council 60%
Housing association 17.5%
Owner occupied 18%
Shared ownership 4.5%

The Master Plan was not solely concerned with housing. There were other objectives:

Employment
Education
Community safety

Town centre
Health
Transport
Community development (which became an objective halfway through the programme)

How was the Master Plan implemented? What effect did it have on residents and local churches? Has a new, cohesive and safer community been created?

To implement the Master Plan, the Peckham Partnership Board was established. A wide range of interests was represented on the Board, reflecting the extent of the regeneration programme and the involvement of private-sector companies and housing associations. In order to secure approximately £60 million of the Government's Single Regeneration Budget (SRB) it was necessary to form a Development Partnership with private-sector housebuilders and housing associations. The regeneration programme began on 1 April 1995 with an estimated seven-year life.

Most of the Single Regeneration Budget money awarded to the project was for physical reconstruction. The demolition of the bulk of the five estates was a massive undertaking, and the decanting and re-housing of residents was a difficult and complex operation. The dedicated team based in offices within the regeneration area, and the Housing Department of Southwark Council, must be given credit for the relatively smooth running of this process. While some tenants could move directly into a new property, the great majority had to be re-housed in other parts of the Borough, either permanently or temporarily. In the initial stages more tenants chose to leave the area permanently. Gradually, as the new streets and houses took shape, more opted to return. In a scheme of this size it was inevitable that it would impact on the Borough as a whole, and especially its housing. Those needing re-housing from the scheme, whether permanent or temporary, had first priority. While it was done in phases, the sheer scale meant that it was not only difficult to find suitable properties, but that the process also had a knock-on effect on the housing waiting list in the Borough.

The noise and dust of demolition added to the stress of living in North Peckham as residents waited to see what they would be offered – an experience that I shared. The hall/vicarage complex was next to Farnborough Way. There was not only the noise and dust, but the whole complex shook as the cement ball smashed into the surrounding blocks. I was one of the last residents to move as the old vicarage was demolished and a new one built on a site next to Udens, the local funeral directors.

Beverly and Elvis and their family were the last to be moved from the North Peckham Estate: 'Windows were dirty and unkempt, communal areas weren't cleaned, rats were all over the place, and we were embarrassed to let family and friends see where we lived. A florist refused to deliver flowers.' Eileen, a resident on the North Peckham Estate for 29 years, echoes their experience: 'It was left open to thieves. There were three attempted burglaries, and no security guards. Refuse collection wasn't so regular and the cleaning of the estate deteriorated. It felt very unsafe, and got worse as people were moved out. Flats weren't secured properly.' North Peckham was a stressful place to live, and became more so as the regeneration programme unfolded.

The whole programme depended on a partnership being formed between the local authority and private housebuilding companies and housing associations, one of which was the Southwark and London Diocesan Housing Association. There was some resentment that housing associations had to be involved for financial reasons (as only housing assocations could draw in Social Housing Grant), but generally the partnership worked well. The Partnership Board was probably a good body to oversee the physical reconstruction aspect of the programme.

An important objective for the regeneration programme was to have mixed tenure, thus ending the monopoly of the local authority. As Steve Joyce, director of the Southwark London Diocesan Housing Association, has written: 'Developing housing with a mixture of tenure such as private housing, and affordable rented housing, is now regarded as a desirable piece of social engineering.'[2] The proportion of private dwellings is 18 per cent. Originally, a proportion of these flats and houses were to be affordable for local tenants. This would have fulfilled the aspirations of some tenants and given greater continuity to the community. However, market prices prevailed and local tenants could not afford them. There is a lingering resentment among some people over this.

The question is, will the homeowners become part of the community? Will they shop in Rye Lane, the main shopping area for Peckham? Will they make a contribution as part of the voluntary sector? Will their children go to local schools? Will they attend local churches? Will tenants and homeowners have, or seek, opportunities for friendship? Will North Peckham become two communities that have little or no contact? Some of the private developments are gated communities. The gates both keep in and keep safe the residents and keep out potential burglars and everyone else. They suggest that the people living there are unlikely to be seeking or welcoming a relationship with local authority and housing association tenants. Some of the private housing has already had more than one owner. Are the new homeowners simply passing through or will they become long-term residents committed to the community? It is too early to judge, but there has been no influx of new home-owning people to St Luke's Church or to any other local church as far as I am aware. Maybe they are not churchgoers or they go else-where. If homeowners continue to pass through, with little or no contact with tenants, that will be a concern, and it will mean the failure of this part of the vision for Peckham.

Community Development

Community Development only became one of the Partnership Objectives halfway through the seven-year life of the programme. Regeneration is never only about bricks and mortar. Community Development, with the empowering of local people that it implies, should have been one of the original objectives, and the recognition of its necessity probably came too late for it to be as effective as it could have been. While the strategy changed to address Community Development Issues, the Partnership Board, in its continuing unchanged composition, was probably not the ideal body to initiate and oversee this work. The one building still to be demolished on the North Peckham Estate is the one containing the workshops and tenants hall, boarded up and unused now for eight years. There is no plan to replace this or any of the other tenants' halls that were demolished. There are other halls within the area, but tenants will not have a hall of their own.

The establishment of a Community Development Trust, run by the Tenants and Residents Forum, never happened. Wherever responsibility lies for this failure, it is a real tragedy. An opportunity to empower local residents has been lost. With the loss of meeting space and failure of the Community Development Trust, the process of regeneration has been a disempowering and disillusioning one for some local residents, and there is a legacy in the community of bitterness and frustration.

The Church

And what of the churches during this massive regeneration pro-gramme? Within the regeneration area, the Anglican churches of St Luke's and St George's, and the North Peckham Baptist Church, remained. The Roman Catholic churches of Our Lady of Sorrows and

St James are both located outside the area. During the process of regeneration the population was often much reduced as tenants were moved out. What effect did this have on church membership? Perhaps, surprisingly, the answer is very little. Indeed, at St Luke's Church, membership increased year by year from 77 in 1996 to its present level of 152. There would appear to be two main reasons for this. The first was a feeling of loyalty to St Luke's, expressed by a number of members who now live outside the area, sometimes a considerable distance away. Eileen, who now lives a mile or so away in Walworth, said this. 'I didn't consider moving to another church. I've got used to the church and community and didn't want to start over again.' Eileen was one of the North Peckham Estate residents who had fought so hard on behalf of tenants during the regeneration process. Her loyalty was to both church and community even though the latter has changed so much. Perhaps remaining at St Luke's provided continuity and stability for her at a time of upheaval and stress.

The second reason for congregational growth has been the increased number of people from West Africa, particularly from Nigeria, Sierra Leone and Ghana, who are practising Christians. Some 70 per cent of the St Luke's membership is now West African.

As far as other local churches are concerned, my impression is that their membership remained stable during the regeneration process and some have grown since 2002, due also, in part, to the greater number of people from West Africa living in the community.

The ethnic diversity of North Peckham has been maintained to the benefit of local churches who rejoice in the diversity of their congregations and the enrichment this brings to them. Increasing church membership has been an unintended consequence of the regeneration programme.

As the bulldozing of the estates went on, so new houses and streets took their place, and the churches had to discover the location and names of these new streets. St Luke's, whose parish covered four of the old estates (the Gloucester Grove Estate was in St George's parish), undertook leaflet drops as each new phase was completed. Delivery to front doors from the street was so much easier and safer than before: no stairwells, no dark corners, no dodgy lifts, and a numbering system that is logical. It is so much easier to find a particular house or flat now. The only place where access to front doors and letterboxes isn't so easy, or is impossible, are the gated communities of the homeowners.

The Master Plan, once drawn up, was rolled out and, like a juggernaut, was unstoppable. Criticisms of the process and of the standard of housebuilding were raised by individuals like Eileen and by the Churches Forum. On behalf of the Churches Forum I raised the issue of soundproofing in the new flats and houses. They have cavity walls that are not very soundproof (unlike the refurbished blocks which have plaster walls and are more soundproof). This would be an on-going nuisance for tenants. The reply was that it met the current building regulations and was a cheaper option than plaster walls. The juggernaut rolled on.

The St Luke's Church building, located at the heart of the five estates, benefited directly from the regeneration programme. The dedicated team working in the area could see that the church grounds would be an eyesore and needed improving. Before, the grounds fitted in with their surroundings, but now they would be a blot on the new landscape. St Luke's now has new railings and a new car-parking surface through SRB funding, and a new hall and garden – through a land-swap deal – enabled the old vicarage/hall complex to be demolished to make way for one of the major new streets in the area.

Amid the chaos of demolition and the stress, anxiety and uncertainty that the whole regeneration process has created for local residents, the churches were centres of calm and stability. The Churches Forum and Christian lay people were part of the process of regeneration, being both supportive and critical where necessary. It was a testing time for the churches as well as all involved in the regeneration of the five estates.

Now it's done

The title of this chapter is 'Now It's Done: The North Peckham Estate after the Makeover'. Well, it's not done yet. There is still one block on the North Peckham Estate and one very large block on the Gloucester Grove Estate to be demolished. Given the massive scale and complexity of the regeneration programme, it's not surprising that it has overrun and that the end is still not in sight. One of the questions posed was: 'Why do it at all?' Refurbishment and improvement of the old five estates would never have been enough to overcome the area's bad reputation. The physical environment needed changing, not only to replace a vision for community living that was increasingly being seen as flawed, but to eradicate a reputation.

The physical environment has been radically altered. Some of the old blocks have been refurbished and improved, to good effect, and where once there were large blocks of flats and stairwells, walkways and balconies, now there are streets and houses and newly planted trees. Is it a safer place to live now? Eileen and Victoria, both quoted earlier, have told me that they felt it to be safer. Victoria has also said this: 'The children seem happier, not as depressed.' As families moved into the new homes, especially in the earlier stages, they must have known the reputation of the North Peckham Estate and been a bit anxious. Bonney, aged 18, moved with his family into a house in Cator Street, one of the old streets of the North Peckham Estate, ten years ago. They had lived in another part of Peckham, but knew the area's reputation. He told me that they were apprehensive at first, but 'we were soon OK. The street is quiet and we aren't living in fear of burglary or mugging.' The crime rate for burglary and mugging has gone down considerably and so has the fear of crime. While this is not necessarily directly attributable to the housing objective, it is a beneficial outcome of it. Further research needs to be done into how housing design may help to reduce crime and the fear of crime.

The regeneration programme wasn't just about housing. There is a new library (an award-winning building), the Peckham Pulse (a swimming pool and healthy-living centre combined), the Lister Health Centre, and new public open spaces: Peckham Square and Sumner Park. The question is: 'What difference will these facilities make to the health, education and leisure activities of local residents?' While the physical environment has been greatly improved and seems to be a safer place to live, it is just as important that these new facilities have a positive impact on local people's lives if the regeneration is to be adjudged a success. These new community facilities were always part of the programme. Whether they are sufficient in number and quality remains to be seen.

North Peckham now has a mixed housing tenure. The old socialist ideal of estates with the local authority as sole landlord has been swept away. One piece of social engineering has been replaced by another. We will have to wait and see if the new community gels. The new mixed tenure has a number of landlords: local authority and housing associations. This may seem like a good idea to some people, and may prove to be so, but it might make the formation and sustainability of tenants' associations harder and common action less likely. Mixed tenure may be thought to be socially desirable, but it might lead to a more fragmented and divided community.

The regeneration programme began in 1995. In November 2000, there came the tragic death of Damilola Taylor on a stairwell in one of the old blocks of the North Peckham Estate. His death caused great shock and anguish in the community. The fact that it happened on part of the old estate seemed to confirm the bad reputation of North Peckham and the rightness of demolishing the estates. There is a memorial to Damilola outside Oliver Goldsmith School, and the Warwick Park Centre was renamed the Damilola Taylor Centre. As well as being permanent reminders of his tragic death, they can, hopefully, encourage us all to strive to make this a better and safer community in which to live.

As parish priest of St Luke's Church, walking down the new streets and between the refurbished blocks, it feels safer and much less edgy. It doesn't feel like a community under siege. Young people are playing in the streets, and people are more visible. Much has been done to change and improve North Peckham and there is more to come – for example, the tram that may be routed down Chandler Way. St Luke's, like all the local churches, will need to remain open and inclusive and alert to the needs and problems faced by local people.

Regeneration has brought improvement, but problems of unemployment, low pay, hardship and low achievement in local schools remain. This isn't a criticism of the regeneration programme, but it is a recognition that all is not well for everyone and that this must not be forgotten in the rush to declare the programme a success.

The future

The regeneration of the North Peckham Estate, the five estates, is nearly complete. Is it now a place where people want to live? Yes: there is anecdotal evidence to suggest that people are beginning to see the area in a more favourable light.

The Peckham programme vision is this: 'Our aim is to continue to work in partnership towards the creation of a sustainable Urban Village in and around Peckham.' How realistic this is remains open to question. The idea of a 'village' seems something of a romantic ideal and nothing to do with the hard realities of inner-city life. In such a diverse community, where life for many residents remains tough and unpredictable, fostering a sense of belonging, common purpose and pride in the community will not be easy. The churches and local residents can't simply wait and see. We will have to work to create a better, safer, more sustainable community where people respect and value one another.

The regeneration of North Peckham has caused massive upheaval and permanent change. Has it all been worth it? The signs are that it has been, though there are lessons that can be learnt that could prove useful for future regeneration schemes, and in particular that community development should be at the heart of any such scheme, otherwise it could be just bricks and mortar, which is never enough.

Notes

1　Wavehill Consulting, 'End of Scheme SRB Evaluation', p. 11.
2　Joyce, Steve, letter to the author, 2006.

7. Up It Goes

The Church Among North Southwark's New Financial District

TIM SCOTT

... seek the welfare of the city where I have sent you into exile, and pray to the LORD on its behalf, for in its welfare you will find your welfare. (Jeremiah 29.7)

Date – 10 October 2004: the licensing service had gone well and the church was full. Now it was Sunday morning and around 25 people were gathered for the Sunday morning Eucharist. I felt rather nervous, particularly as I was not sure how things were 'normally done' in the parish. I remember thinking that the congregation were probably as nervous as I was, a large piano between me and them, and a setting where there seemed little or no visible response to what I did and said. I wondered if this was a sign of the congregation feeling powerless in the face of change. Here was a new parish priest, with all the uncertainty which that brings, and a congregation set within a local community facing unprecedented change. An area that had previously seen an influx of industry followed by its decline, now faces new commercial, financial, tourist and cultural developments combined with a rapid increase in already high housing costs. This area of London is commonly called Bankside, a small area of North Southwark, and for the purposes of this chapter it is defined as stretching from Blackfriars Bridge to Southwark Bridge and south to Southwark tube station. The geographically small parish of Christ Church covers a significant proportion of Bankside as well as some of the streets west of Blackfriars Bridge and south of Southwark tube station.

A changing context: some examples

When I describe to anyone who doesn't know London very well the area that I work in, I say 'The Tate Modern is in the parish' – which tells people that we're just over the river from St Paul's Cathedral. It often also brings a response such as 'How lucky you are', or 'Are you the chaplain to the Tate?' (which I am not, although I do have some links there, and when the Bishop of Woolwich came last year for his visitation he was taken on a tour of some of the galleries).

The Tate Modern is a museum of modern art housed in a converted power station. The work of converting the Bankside power station to a museum of modern art began in 1995 and was completed in 2000. There had been a coal-fired station on the site since 1891, but that building was damaged in World War Two. Work on the new building, designed by Gilbert Scott, began in 1948, but not without controversy. There were significant objections to the design of the new building, not least that the power station, with its large tower, would interrupt the view of St Paul's Cathedral, whose vista had been opened up by wartime bombing. (It was also argued that the fumes would drift across the river and damage the stonework of St Paul's.) The second objection was that such a large building in this location would not fit with the intention, under the Abercrombie Plan for post-war reconstruction, to create more open space and recreational areas in this part of London. However, the then Minister for Town and Country Planning, Lewis Silkin, overruled the objections and granted permission, with the proviso that the power station should be oil-fired rather than coal-fired in order to prevent damage to St Paul's. The issues were debated in Parliament and in the Lords the scheme was 'likened to "introducing an alligator into a water lily pond" but the Lord Chancellor, Viscount Jowett, early to appreciate the beauty of the power station, retorted "this may be the largest and most beautiful lily in the pond"'.[1]

In 2006 some of the objections to the new skyscraper commercial and residential buildings being proposed in the area are remarkably similar, in particular with regard to sight lines from St Paul's and the need for green and open space and recreational facilities. Whether the emerging buildings will be the 'largest and most beautiful lily in the pond' remains to be seen! The Tate Modern itself is now planning a huge new extension which will be a centrepiece for the developing cultural quarter of the South Bank, which is set to become a focus of attraction for those visiting the 2012 Olympics based in east London. The change from power station to cultural centre in some ways epitomizes the extent and nature of change in this area of London.

After World War Two the Bankside area of Southwark close to the Thames saw much change with some large industrial firms leaving the area (e.g. the Marine engineers John Rennie) and others moving in (such as Sainsbury's). All of the central elements of Sainsbury's operations were run from Bankside, much of it in buildings adjacent to Christ Church. However, with the increasing containerization of transport, ships getting larger, and the subsequent closure of the Port of London, manufacturing industry in the Bankside area began to suffer. Many of the wharves closed and Sainsbury's was deprived of access to many of its raw materials. New demand for a speedy supply of fresh foods meant that by 1973 Sainsbury's warehousing, distribution and food processing had moved from the area, and recently their administrative head office moved to Holborn. The two Sainsbury's buildings next to Christ Church have been bought by Land Securities and there have been tentative proposals for a major commercial and residential development on these sites (possibly 32 storeys). On another of the previous Sainsbury's sites in the area the Dubai-based Jumeira Group have signed an agreement with the Beetham Organization to create a new £600-million 51-storey luxury hotel, with additional apartments and penthouses on the upper floors, and some 'affordable' homes in an adjacent building. The hotel is planned to open in 2011, just in time for the Olympics, and is a further example of the vast change and globalization of this area.

Residents at the new luxury hotel will overlook the Thames in one direction and in another the building that was formerly the home of Express Newspapers: The *Daily Express* moved from Fleet Street to the Bankside area of Blackfriars in 1989. It was sold to Richard Desmond in 2000, and in 2004 (together with *OK!* and *Now!* magazines) moved to its present location in Lower Thames Street in the City of London. Their old building in Bankside is currently let to United Business Media and has just recently been sold to a private investor. While the publishing group IPC Media will still remain in the area, relocating into new offices developed by Land Securities, the long history of printing in the area is coming to an end. I still hear stories from those who worked in the printing presses down Blackfriars Road, and in Christ Church itself there is a memorial sculpture by Ian Walters, who died recently, called 'The Wapping Memorial'. It depicts the struggles of the print workers at the time of the move to Wapping in the 1980s. Christ Church hosted many of the trades unions meetings and still hosts occasional social functions for retired members of the print and communication workers unions.

Next door to Christ Church there is a disused building with the fading inscription 'Society of Operative Printers and Assistants', a stark reminder of the strength of the printing tradition in the area. Two doors away from this is the wonderfully named pub, the Paper Moon, and a few doors along is the Mad Hatter Hotel, once a hat factory, where, it is said, the process of making hats drove the workers mad. The present frontage has a Dickensian character to it and is a reminder of the historic nature of the area and the wonderfully descriptive names. There is for instance a pub in Blackfriars Road called the Laughing Gravy, either named after a Laurel and Hardy film about a dog called Laughing Gravy, or named after the 1920s slang expression for alcohol, depending on which story you prefer to believe. One of the fears is that the vast change going on in the area will result in a characterless community that forgets or destroys not only the buildings, but also the memories of the past.

Christ Church

In 1625 a local businessman named John Marshall died. Little is known about him except that he was a prosperous merchant who was also concerned with the welfare of clergy. In his will, his 13 trustees were charged with 'building for £700 a new church with churchyard in Southwark to be called Christ Church, and the payment of the stipend of a minister'.[2] The church was built in 1670, but began to sink in the boggy ground close to the Thames and had to be rebuilt in 1738, this time on piles. The building lasted until 1941 when it was bombed, and a stone cross marks the place where the cross from the tower fell. The present church was built in 1960 and is still owned by the present-day trustees of the Marshall's Charity who generously support the maintenance of the building and the cost of some of the ministry here.

Christ Church has always sought to be a locally rooted church serving the local community. In the 1850s the resident population of the parish was around 17,000, and the church was therefore serving a substantial number of residents. A hundred years later, the resident population of the area had reduced to around 2,000 and the area had changed from a major residential area to an industrial one. Thus the new building of Christ Church opened in 1960 as an industrial centre. This was the brainchild of Allan Weaver, the rector during the 1950s who had built up a particular rapport with people working in the industry of the area. On his retirement, the South London Industrial Mission (SLIM) moved its headquarters to Christ Church, and in 1967 the then Bishop of Woolwich, John Robinson, appointed Peter Challen to be both rector of Christ Church and senior chaplain of SLIM, thus integrating SLIM with Christ Church.

The intention to relate faith to work in the developing industrial context is graphically illustrated in the stained-glass windows to be found in Christ Church. One set were installed in 1959 and another in 1984. They depict scenes from the industrial life of the area from the days of the first church in 1670 to the present day.

While the windows provide a unique historical record they are now somewhat dated. The nature of the area has changed and is changing dramatically, so the images of printing presses and Sainsbury's no longer reflect the present climate of commercial, financial, tourist and cultural developments. The post of senior chaplain of SLIM no longer exists, and I was appointed in October 2004 as both rector of Christ Church and the Bishop of Southwark's Adviser on Regeneration. SLIM moved out of Christ Church in October 2005. The challenges and the context are new, but the principle of engagement with, and service of, the local area continues. But it is now a global context, and property development is the most obvious industry.

This was brought home to me within my first week in the parish when I was invited to attend a meeting in the church hall at Christ Church. The meeting was an opportunity for local residents to meet representatives of one of the large international developers. They brought with them initial plans, drawings and models of a possible skyscraper building on the doorstep of Christ Church. To this day, I am not sure who called the meeting, but I was delighted that Christ Church was being used as a place for open discussion about some of the crucial issues facing the community. The meeting was well attended and local residents expressed their deep concerns, fears and anger in the midst of such large-scale, tall-building development. Clearly there was a feeling among many residents of a 'takeover' of their community. It was assumed and hoped that I would be against all development, and when I made one contribution that indicated that something the developer had done – and proposed to do – might be good, helpful and worthwhile, I was immediately and vociferously shot down. Very real anger was expressed when I did not come out against all development. I went away from that meeting somewhat battered and confused and realizing that I had some hard thinking to do about the role of Christ Church at this time in the history of North Southwark, and about my role as rector. I have also come to realize that sometimes there is a flurry of activity, as around that meeting, which in the end comes to nothing. Now, two years on, it is no clearer whether that particular development will take place or in what form. And yet the pace of change in the area means we cannot assume every flurry of activity will come to nothing. In a global setting, in which decisions to do with development may be based on the state of the money markets or what's happening in Shanghai, Mumbai or New York, it is difficult, if not impossible, to know which flurries of activity will come to anything.

One flurry of activity that *has* come to something is the development at Christ Church of a 'Faith in Regeneration Project'. This emerged as the result of a major study of North Southwark and North Lambeth (called the London South Central area) commissioned by two groups of Anglican churches. An identified need in this area was the high level of child poverty, and a project was developed through Welcare, an organization working on social issues within the Diocese of Southwark, which resulted in someone being appointed to work with faith communities over a period of three years to develop five projects addressing the issue of child poverty. We have been able to provide the office space for this project at Christ Church and it has added an important dimension to our work. It is a reminder of the constant danger of the poorest in our communities being pushed aside. While engagement with the vast property and commercial developers is necessary and provides the opportunity to shape developments whose impact will be enormous, it is often the encounter with those most marginalized that has a significant impact on our thinking and development of vision.

I remember very vividly visiting an exhibition at the Tate Modern soon after I arrived. Beneath the cranes of the big developers dominating the skyline there was an exhibition entitled 'Shrinking Childhoods'. The art displayed was the result of a series of workshops held over the summer with collaboration between Kids Company and Tate Modern involving more than 1,000 children aged between four and twenty-one. It depicts the experience of children whose lives are dominated by abuse, violence and poverty. The location of the exhibition in portacabins, with the tower of the Tate Modern on one side and the huge cranes of a large commercial development on the other, provided a graphic image with which to judge much of the urban regeneration emerging in the area and its effect on the life of local people and the long-term well-being of the whole community.

The local becomes ever more important in a global context. Members of our small, ethnically diverse local Sunday congregation are involved in tenants' groups, while others take an active part in local grassroots issues, not least the need for good local shopping facilities for those who live in the area. Another concern is good television reception, which is at present severely interfered with by the building of some of the large tower blocks. Among the organizations to which we offer office space there is a local newspaper very involved in local community issues. We also offer space to the Confraternity of St James, which leads pilgrimages to Santiago de Compostela; an Alexander Technique teacher; a Ghanaian pastor; a racial equality and employment project; a dance and drama therapy group; and worship space for a largely Nigerian congregation. Part of my role as rector has been to attempt to create a context in which things can flourish and new initiatives emerge. Dance and drama therapy workshops are being developed. Together with other churches in the area, a winter night-shelters project is being planned for those who are homeless. Another very different development is a series of lunchtime concerts at Christ Church, possible partly because we have a choir that practises each week in the church, and partly because we have a pianist who plays for our Sunday worship who is a Fellow at the Guildhall School of Music and Drama.

With a residential population of around 1,700 people and upwards of 20,000 who work in the parish, what we do during the week is crucial. We keep the church open as much as possible and the visitors' book indicates that it is much appreciated and well used as people come in seeking space, silence and an oasis. One entry in the visitors' book epitomizes many of the sentiments expressed: 'Thank you. Lovely to find the church open. An open invitation to pray. Thank you.' The gardens surrounding the church, which are owned by Southwark Council and managed by the Bankside Open Spaces Trust, provide a green oasis which, as we have seen from our discussion of open space in the first part of this chapter, is crucial to people's well-being. While keeping an eye on the bigger picture (which includes liaising with the London Development Agency, which has just moved into the first of the major new buildings to be completed in the parish), it is also important to see the impact of the small and the local, of which Christ Church gardens is an example. Southwark Parks Department is putting new signs in their parks, and we have been working with them, Bankside Open Spaces Trust and local residents on the actual wording to go on the information board. In particular it has been important to include on the signage something of the history of the area and the history of the church. The church, present and local since 1670, holds the memories, hopes and fears of many generations, including the present one. It understands the need for a 'public' dimension to life, whether it is public space or symbolic activity at crucial points in personal or corporate life. But it is not the only place where symbolism or ritual takes place, as I discovered in a particular way in the autumn of last year.

Symbol, ritual and God

In September last year an invitation arrived to attend the 'topping out' ceremony of one of the Land Securities developments in the area, Bankside One. Topping out happens when the last beam is placed at the top of a building. Its origin is obscure, but the ceremony is common in Germany and America. In America, when a sky-scraper is completed, the last girder to be hoisted is painted white and signed by all the workmen involved. A leafy tree branch and the US flag are tied to it. Toasts are drunk and sometimes the workmen are treated to a meal. In other buildings the ceremony focuses on the bedding of the last block of masonry or brick. The ceremony is akin to the practice of placing a newspaper or coins under the foundation stone of a building, or to ship naming and launching ceremonies, and it might be of similar antiquity. Originally the ceremony might have been carried out to placate the gods, and to have been to shield the building from harm. It is also said that in ancient times, if people liked the building, then the architect was praised at the ceremony; but that if the building was not popular then the architect was killed! There was no such drastic event on this occasion, but there was the ceremonial laying of a final piece of cement followed by speeches, food and drinks. The ceremony was a symbolic ritual of the structural completion of the building and prepared the way for the internal work necessary for the forthcoming move of IPC Media into the building.

On my desk I have a square paperweight containing the outline of the Bankside One building that I was given at the topping-out ceremony and it serves as a reminder of that event. It was, however, the view from the top of the 13-floor building that I remember most clearly. I had a real sense of the financial and commercial sector of London moving south of the river. I also looked over and saw the church in the distance, surrounded by trees and garden, and I looked down on ancient almshouses that had at their rear a wonder-ful oasis of a garden, now overlooked by office blocks, the Tate Modern and some high-cost luxury flats. Speaking with one of the long-term residents of the almshouses I had already heard of the feeling that many local residents are experiencing, of being domi-nated by the pace and scale of building.

As I walked back to Christ Church to conduct our Thursday lunchtime Eucharist, I reflected on what I had experienced and also on the tradition of radical engagement that Christ Church had deep within its tradition. The context might be different, but the need for discerning the struggle of the gospel and the presence of God in all that was happening was still of crucial importance. I was greeted at the door of the church by a loyal and faithful member of the congregation who himself lives in the almshouses that I had just looked down on from the topping-out ceremony. Now, in the Eucharist, I was to break bread and share wine with him and with about 12 others, and I was reminded of our task to hear the cry of the poor and seek the welfare of the city.

The weekly lunchtime Eucharist at Christ Church has grown from single figures to regularly 12 to 15 people. It offers a moment of space and reflection for people who live or work in the area and those who may be tourists or simply passing the door. It is an opportunity for people to come, and, in the words of Psalm 46.10: 'Be still, and know that I am God!' It is a symbolic occasion that enables people to bring the reality of their lives into the presence of the transcendent.

That same process of bringing reality into the presence of the transcendent was very evident when we held an Open Day, focusing on the theme of peace. It was largely organized by one of our churchwardens, who drew together resources from the internet and work from the children and young people of the church and displayed them around the church. Candles were kept alight and others were available for people to light. The symbolic action of lighting a candle can be an accessible way for people to respond to often unarticulated needs. As people walk into the church for services or when it is simply open, there are candles available for lighting. We have Stations of the Cross along the side of the church, enabling people to reflect on issues of life and death, hope and love. On the church walls there are displays from the work of our Sunday school. People might also see through into the church hall where one of the 'Urban Seminars' I am co-ordinating in my role as Regeneration Adviser might be taking place. These are an attempt to provide opportunity for discussion about the rapidly changing context of London as a whole, not least in terms of demography, governance and power. Our hope is that as people walk through the doors of Christ Church they will experience work, reflection and prayer for the welfare of the city, and be able to reflect on the deep things of God and of our life together.

What does the future hold?

In May 2006 the Church of England published, in conjunction with the Methodist Church, a report called *Faithful Cities: A Call for Celebration, Vision and Justice*, in which it highlights the important contribution of faith within the life of cities and asks the question: 'What makes a good city?'

The national briefing on the *Faithful Cities* document for the Church of England dioceses throughout the country was held at Christ Church in June. In the course of the meeting someone who was homeless and in some considerable distress came into the church and, after listening for a while to the presentation, interrupted and began to tell us the reality of life for him. It was a poignant moment and highlighted for me some of the questions that we will need to address at Christ Church as we seek to proclaim the gospel and seek the welfare of the city at this time in this place. Briefly these are:

- Who belongs in Southwark and who does Southwark belong to?
- Will attention be given to the 'public' dimension or realm, without which community will not flourish and a soulless concrete desert will be created?
- What infrastructure of housing and services will be developed to ensure the poorest in our community are not simply displaced?
- How can Christ Church develop partnerships and a vision that takes into account its geographical location, with good transport links, at the centre of a global city?

Two years after my service of induction, with which I started this chapter, I have more questions than answers. But maybe that is always true as we seek to follow the call of our Lord to seek the welfare of the city.

Further reading

Commission on Urban Life and Faith, *Faithful Cities: A Call for Celebration, Vision and Justice*, Church House Publishing/Methodist Publishing House, London, 2006.

Davey, A., *Urban Christianity and Global Order: Theological Resources for an Urban Future*, SPCK, London, 2001.

Reilly, L. and Marshall, G., *The Story of Bankside*, London Borough of Southwark, London, 2001.

Notes

1 Reilly, L. and Marshall, G., *The Story of Bankside*, London Borough of Southwark, London, 2001.

2 'John Marshall and his Will': a briefing from the Marshall's Charity.

8. Creating Space

The Aylesbury Estate and the InSpire Project

GILES GODDARD

Enlarge the site of your tent, and let the curtains of your habitations be stretched out; do not hold back, lengthen your cords and strengthen your stakes. (Isaiah 54.2)

Following the snail trails

The drummers led the procession. They were from Creative Routes, a project run by and for people with mental health problems. Following them, as darkness fell, was a long line of lanterns, glowing in the dusk. A six-foot long shark, light flickering out of its open mouth. A star. Another star. A batch of Chinese lanterns held high on bamboo poles. A moon, held high by a ten-year-old child who had spent the last three weeks making it. Flowers, another fish, a space rocket. All constructed carefully by people of all ages, tissue paper stretched across willow and varnished, carried by mums and grans and kids and dads. African and English, Turkish and Canadian. Taxi drivers, unemployed people, classroom assistants, healthworkers.

We walked slowly from InSpire along the streets on to the Aylesbury Estate, between Missenden and Latimer blocks, stopping in the new children's play area to pick up more from the Aylesbury Youth Project, and back through the Octavia Hill Estate into the garden by the churchyard. By the time we reached the garden, darkness had fallen. The procession climbed the mound in the centre. From the gates of the church I watched the massed lanterns lifted high in the night, surrounded by the lights of the Portland Street tower blocks and accompanied by the drums of Creative Routes.

This, I thought, was what we made InSpire for.

Scroll back to September 1998. The residents of the Aylesbury Estate are in a mixture of despair and hope.

Despair, because their bid to Europe for major funding had just been turned down. The bid was carefully put together and confidently submitted, after guidance from the government. It offered a chance for the increasingly shabby and run-down estate to escape from its descending spiral, a noxious mix of fear of crime, abuse, and physical neglect of the estate. It had the support of tenants, the local authority and the government. It failed.

Hope, because a new initiative has just been announced, and because the Prime Minister made the Aylesbury Estate his first stop after the 1997 election, promising that things would get better. As a first step towards that, the Department of the Environment was announcing a pilot scheme called 'New Deal for Communities' (NDC) which would, it was hoped, offer some of the poorest and most deprived areas of the UK a chance to turn themselves round. Local people were to be given the opportunity to bid for up to £57 million to spend over ten years, on the priorities *they* identified, and to bring about the transformations *they* needed. What could be more full of hope?

The congregation of St Peter's Church, Walworth, were wondering what the future held for them. The building, a Grade 1 listed church by Sir John Soane, was in a poor state. The boilers were reaching the end of their life. The crypt, which had in the past acted as a thriving social club, was virtually derelict; the gutters from the roof were blocked and sent water straight into the crypt, which stank of damp and dereliction; snail trails ran round the bars, and the churchwardens were loyally keeping going the social club (which was scarcely representative of the surrounding area). The Sunday congregation had been running on empty for some time, despite the hard work of a few key members, and was unsure about its future. There was £70 in the bank account and an outstanding oil bill for £600.

A key word: 'struggle'. Jean Bartlett, a grandmother on the estate, had the care of her young grandchild during the day. She realized that there were no care facilities available anywhere for the thousands of young mothers in the area. 'There was nothing for us,' she says. 'Everything we did we had to fight for. When I set up "Little Tykes", no one would listen at first.' The Aylesbury, built mainly in the early 1970s, system-built low- and medium-rise housing, had quickly stopped being a place of hope and become a place that was 'notorious' (that word so often applied to poor estates) for its crime and drug problems, for the teenage pregnancy statistics, for high unemployment and for poor health: a nexus of apparently intractable problems.

A key word: struggle. Toro Erogbogbo, now one of the churchwardens at St Peter's, remembers: 'No one would talk to you in the street. When another member of the church saw you, they'd turn away.'

The damp and the cold as winter set in filled me, as the new parish priest, with anxiety. The building seemed too big for the congregation and the churchyard was a wilderness. The people of St Peter's seemed stuck in a position where all they could do was repeat what they knew, and hope that somehow things would get better.

I took up the post of rector in September 1998. I'd been given the specific responsibility, as part of my appointment, of working with the people of the Aylesbury Estate to support them in the plans for their homes and their communities. But what did this mean? What were we going to do with the building? What part of the gospel of love were we called to be offering, here in Walworth? How could we as a congregation respond to the clear and present needs around us and in our midst?

Light into darkness?

One of the most useful maxims I've ever been given is: 'time spent in reconnaissance is seldom wasted'. For us, as a church, the advice we received was to investigate the current situation: to find out who lived around us, what their priorities were, and what potential existed within the church.

With the help of and funding from Business in the Community, we carried out an independent audit of local needs, and we interviewed residents and members of the church. We sent out 500 questionnaires and had a good return. We talked to community groups and local service providers. And we reviewed the statistics.

We discovered that:

- Faraday Ward was among the 10 per cent most deprived in the UK.
- Some 33 per cent of residents were on Income Support and 23 per cent were lone parents.
- Seven out of ten unemployed people had not worked for over two years.
- Key health and education indicators were among the poorest in the UK.
- Some 66 per cent of local residents identified themselves as coming from an ethnic minority.

Key areas where the need for help and support was identified were:

- Basic skills.
- English as a second language training, and IT training.
- Careers advice/job seeking.
- Parental support.

None of this was surprising; it confirmed the preconceptions we had about the parish.

But further investigation of the situation showed us that the superficial statistics told only a tiny part of the story: they could be seen as the tip of the iceberg, exposed to the battering of high winds and storms. The impression began to form of something profoundly solid and deeply impressive, below the waterline and invisible. We had an idea of that from the residents of the Aylesbury Estate who came to church, many of whom had lived on the estate for over 30 years. But the reconnaissance we carried out gave weight and breadth to our impressions, and changed the way we understood our responsibility as a parish church.

A 'Mutual Aid Survey' was carried out in early 1999. The Borough of Southwark commissioned a project to identify the extent of 'mutual aid' that took place on the Aylesbury Estate. It uncovered some statistics that surprised us:

- 90 per cent of people gave help or support to a neighbour.
- 81 per cent received help or support from a neighbour.
- 47 per cent had lived on the Estate for more than 10 years.
- 20 per cent gave or received help from a relative also living on the Estate.
- Three-quarters were in some sort of regular, routine, informal helping relationship.
- 18 per cent attended a place of worship locally.
- 18 per cent were involved in their tenants' association.
- 63 per cent wanted to return there after any redevelopment.

In other words, the Aylesbury did not conform to the stereotype of a run-down, inner-city estate. While for some people, clearly, the sense of isolation was strong, there also existed a diverse, confident and supportive community, unsung and unacknowledged: a community that had not had the chance to raise its head above the parapet; a community that had been characterized by struggle rather than success, by crime instead of creativity.

This became apparent in our investigations. Because, overwhelmingly, when people were asked what they thought the area needed, they asked for a place to meet, a place for learning, and somewhere for arts and creativity.

We realized that one of the problems for Aylesbury residents was that the community as a whole had few meeting places, that those that existed were small and shabby tenants' halls with limited access, and that people living on and around the estate had scarcely any opportunities to develop the other, less quantifiable aspects of living in South London. A strong series of communities lived around here, but with few chances to express themselves.

We had a semi-derelict building. As a listed building, and the best-preserved John Soane church, it represented both a privilege and a responsibility. Having begun to identify needs, we commissioned feasibility studies, asking our architects to provide a space big enough for 150 people to meet, together with smaller spaces for different activities.

It was a fundamental part of our brief that the worship space, remarkable in its beauty and offering a space for performance and prayer, should remain unaltered. But the crypt was, as crypts tend to be, full of arches and brickwork, so that no space existed large enough for more than ten people to meet comfortably.

The plans, as they emerged, were dramatic: clearing the whole crypt back to its fundamental structure, removing the post-war accretions, opening up the lightwells to bring in natural light, creating north–south and east–west vistas, exposing the original brickwork and opening up spaces for people to meet, dance, talk, create, learn and flourish. The plans offered nothing less than a transformation of a space originally intended (literally) for death into a space for life. They built on the crypt's history. In 1895 Canon William Horsley cleared the crypt of the 'two hundred and fifty bodies strewn about the crypt in a most insanitary fashion according to the customs of our forebears' and began to use it for school meals. Since then it had acted as a soup kitchen, as an air raid shelter (and took a direct hit, with many deaths resulting), and as a social club.

The cost of the transformation, apart from the £1.5 million we had to raise, would be the removal of four massive brick pillars and the opening up of a brick circle. The opposition of the Georgian Group was strong, and we knew that the road towards the realization of our plans would be complicated.

It was always clear to me that the process of developing the project would be as important as the end result. It was through the process that we brought people together, that we discovered the facts about the area, and that we identified a strategy for trying to meet local needs. It was through the process that the church and the local community began to rediscover some of the fundamental connections that had been weakened, and to build new links that crossed boundaries and opened up conversations.

At the heart of the project was the awareness that the whole area was to be completely transformed over the next ten years. The NDC proposals were for a total demolition and rebuild of the Aylesbury Estate. Although these proposals were later rejected by a clear majority of tenants, at the time that we were bringing the project into reality there was a clear assumption that there would be extreme upheaval for local residents. The phased construction programme meant that communities would be moved together, but in spite of that, the estate would be a building site for ten years.

In addition, this part of London is undergoing fundamental changes – the City is reaching further and further south of the River Thames, and the Elephant and Castle, only 500 yards from our parish boundary, is also to be completely redeveloped over the next ten years.

As we saw it, we needed to provide a place of continuity in the midst of massive change: a place of celebration, of excellence, and of light. It needed to be somewhere that people could rely on, and somewhere that felt good, like a place of welcome, and was perceived as somewhere that hadn't been cobbled together on the cheap and funded badly. It needed to be somewhere that people could be proud of, somewhere people could leave feeling better than when they arrived.

Gradually, through research, analysis, conversation, dreaming and praying, the vision for the place emerged. The working group charged with the project came up with a mission statement:

> Our mission is to build up this community, seek justice for people on the edge and serve those in need in Walworth and beyond.

And from the mission statement came the aim, and the name:

> The name?
> 'InSpire', with a strapline – 'learning, arts, community'
> The aim?
> InSpire aims to be a centre for learning where local people can creatively and imaginatively obtain new skills, increase their self-confidence and develop a sense of community.

Upwards from underground

For the people of St Peter's the next two years were the busiest part of the project. We had a triple focus:

1 To build up our relationship as a church with the people of the parish. As well as the Aylesbury Estate, the parish contains the Octavia Hill Estates which were, until 2006, owned by the Church Commissioners. Our involvement with both areas was not as strong as it might be, and Benny Hazlehurst, the Diocesan Estates Outreach Officer, helped us to get involved.

Among other things, we organized church-based meetings for

Aylesbury residents who might be anxious about the NDC plans and their impact on people's homes. I also took up a place on the NDC board, becoming vice-chair for three years.

We offered meeting spaces and support for the new Octavia Hill Tenants' and Residents' Association, which was formed when the Church Commissioners proposed letting their flats at market value.

We organized the Jubilee and the Millennium Festivals, both opportunities for the people of the parish to come together, involving a huge variety of local groups and including a procession of big puppets made by Kids Company with a marching band up the Walworth Road.

2 **To develop the plans for InSpire**. The conservation bodies – English Heritage, the Georgian Group, the Borough of Southwark's Planning Department, the Council for the Care of Churches and the Diocesan Advisory Committee – were all involved in the development of the plans. We worked hard to ensure that the qualities of the building were enhanced through our plans, and were pleased to be opening up parts of the place that had never been seen or that had been obscured by ugly post-war partitioning. For instance, in the main hall, which would be created by removing four pillars, we proposed leaving two columns at the west end, creating an arcade and giving a clear idea of what had been there previously. And the east–west axis along the north side of the building would be completely opened up and stripped back to become a café, with the vaulting contributing to the atmosphere.

But the changes we required met with some opposition; a Consistory Court was held by the Chancellor of the Diocese, with whom lay the authority for approving our proposals. After a full hearing of both sides of the argument, the Chancellor wrote his judgment. He recognized that there was a loss of fabric and that some of the nineteenth-century brickwork would be disrupted, but, taking into account the proposed uses of the place, seeing that without the changes a development that met local needs as effectively would not be possible, and acknowledging that some of the changes would enable the building to be seen and experienced in new ways, he granted approval.

3 **To fundraise**. The original estimate for the conversion was around £700,000. As is the way of these things, it increased to a capital cost of £1.3 million including fees. In order to ensure that something happened within InSpire once we had completed it, we needed revenue funding for the first three years: a further £300,000. Therefore the target was £1.6 million.

A good business plan, clear aims and objectives and strong local support were crucial for our fundraising. Our involvement with Aylesbury NDC demonstrated that the funding we were seeking would be for the whole community, not just for the church. We affirmed this by dropping the original name proposal ('The St Peter Centre') and creating 'InSpire – the Crypt at St Peter's Ltd' as a separate company, with representatives on its management committee from both community and church. It has to be said that, despite this, there was still some mistrust from residents, but fortunately that was outweighed by others who understood what we were trying to do.

One of the first donations received was from the Archbishop of Canterbury (then Archbishop Carey). The Church Urban Fund provided early confirmation of a capital grant, then other small local trusts began to show their support; and then some larger grants came in – from UKOnline, the Single Regeneration Budget, NDC, and the Bridge House Trust. Other charities supported us too – the Sainsbury family trusts and the Wates Foundation. The National Lottery's Community Fund provided £250,000, and gradually we approached our target.

The parish made its contribution too. A derelict church hall was sold to the Diocese for the provision of a new parsonage, and the money we received from that sale was put into the funding for InSpire.

After about two years' hard work there was a gap of only £200,000. One afternoon, the funeral was held in church of one of our much loved local councillors. The new leader of the council was there. After the funeral I showed him the derelict crypt; the council caught the vision of InSpire and the gap was closed.

The 'InSpire' spiral

InSpire was dedicated by the Archbishop of Canterbury on 31 October 2003, after a fraught and complicated year of renovation and construction. With the paint still wet the Centre swung into action. One of the best decisions we took was to include revenue funding in the fundraising. We therefore had a Centre Manager, an Outreach Co-ordinator and an IT Co-ordinator in place.

The speed with which InSpire became a key part of the local community was remarkable. With the support of Southwark Council (who immediately began to use it for meetings and conferences), with a café which, although not quite up to the standard we were hoping for, was offering good food at reasonable prices, and with state of the art IT and close co-operation with partners including

Sure Start, the NDC and the Prince's Trust, our dream of synergy and imagination began to become real.

We aimed to be both rooted and creative. One of the most constructive initiatives has been the close partnership with the Prince's Trust, which offers a 12-week course around confidence-building, teamwork and practical skills to 'NEETS' – young people who are not in employment, education or training. The English as a Second Language and IT courses are well subscribed. These are run closely alongside the more obviously creative work – music, art and drama – so that the same people are involved in activities beyond their original intentions. Jade, for instance, started on the Prince's Trust course and is now training in childcare, having helped out at the children's Summer School.

In November 2005 we opened '2InSpire'. It's on the Aylesbury Estate, in a specially equipped performance space that had not realized its potential since its creation at considerable cost ten years ago. 2InSpire hosts the Aylesbury Choir and line dancing. It also does detailed and intensive work around music and dance with young people on the estate and is about to start an NVQ in hairdressing in response to the requests of those same young people.

I take from conversations with Ann Morisy the idea of churches offering a place of 'alternative performance', a place beyond the imperative of 'profit, power and status'. Without intending to, it seems that that is what's happened at InSpire. Although it's not directly associated with the church – many see it as simply sharing premises – our underlying intention to offer a place where people can 'creatively and imaginatively obtain new skills, increase their self-confidence and develop a sense of community' has led to precisely that sense of alternative performance, with people meeting in different ways on different levels, across the boundaries of class, age, gender, sexual orientation, and ethnicity. We have good links with the Southwark-funded lesbian and gay group, who make their carnival floats in InSpire, and with the over-60s bingo group.

Although the Aylesbury residents voted against redevelopment in 2004, since then it has become apparent that because the buildings are reaching the end of their life, a full demolition and redevelopment will have to happen. The major disruptions originally predicted will come to pass and the residents of Phase 1 are beginning to be moved out.

Sitting at the heart of InSpire it is easy to get things out of proportion, but we have begun to offer the place of continuity we hoped to offer as redevelopment begins. People involved at InSpire see it as a place they can be proud of, and a place that offers hope and constancy in a time of change.

New life is symbolized by the churchyard, which was derelict but has now become a community garden. Canon Horsley kept monkeys in the rectory garden in 1896 for the enjoyment of the people who used the new park he created in the churchyard. We've called the new community garden the Monkey Park in recognition of his efforts.

How has InSpire affected the church itself? The church's own mission statement begins 'We aim to be open, caring and prayerful'. It is difficult to say what the direct connections have been, but the congregation is larger and more confident than it was when we started. The church building is back at the heart of the community, the receptionist of InSpire now comes to church every Sunday, and the parish administrator works very closely with InSpire. Members of the church work in InSpire and attend its courses, and people from InSpire come into church to work, to play and to pray.

The partnership has been a dramatic outworking of the church's sense of its own mission. Put at its simplest, our intention was to serve our local community. Through providing InSpire we are putting our building and our resources at the service of local people. This is one way in which we try to live out the gospel, here, in South London.

Who knows what, in 100 years' time, will have taken the place of InSpire, or whether St Peter's will still be a church. In the meantime we take heart from the outworking of the vision of alternative performance.

A mosaic course is run at InSpire by a local artist who lives on the Octavia Hill Estate. Topps Tiles held a mosaic competition, and the pieces made were entered. One piece was made by an Aylesbury resident who is also a refugee. The judge's comments on his entry perhaps sum up the meaning of InSpire:

The indoor wall piece is one of very few portraits ever submitted for the award and what a splendid piece of work it is. Unfussy but wonderfully expressive, set just off centre using a perfectly balanced colour scheme. I think it is the head of Jesus but apologise if I am wrong. Very well done indeed, this impressive portrait wins the award.

Further reading

Morisy, A., *Journeying Out: A New Approach to Christian Mission*, Continuum (Morehouse), London, 2004.

Simmons, M. (ed.), *Street Credo*, Lemos & Crane, London, 2000.

9. Redeeming Sacred Space

St John's, Angell Town

MARTIN CLARK

In the fourth year the foundation of the house of the LORD was laid, in the month of Ziv. In the eleventh year, in the month of Bul, which is the eighth month, the house was finished in all its parts, and according to all its specifications. (1 Kings 6.37–38)

The parish church of St John the Evangelist, Angell Town, in Brixton in south-west London, stands on a well-tended island of green, on the edge of the Angell Town Estate. You would not guess, were you to look at it now, unless you had a particularly keen eye for evidence of ecclesiastical decay, that there was anything unusual about this church building. It consists of a light and airy worship area in the nave; and the east end of the building, originally the chancel, has been converted to form a nursery, serving the local community. Although the statistics indicate that Angell Town remains one of the most deprived parts of the Anglican Diocese of Southwark, with high levels of teenage pregnancy, domestic violence, single parent-hood, drug abuse, and incidence of gun and knife crime, outwardly the estate is neat and tidy, with little evidence of litter or graffiti, and composed largely of newly built low-rise houses and flats.

As recently as 1998 the appearance was very different. The estate then consisted largely of massive four-storey-high blocks of flats. They had been designed and built in the early 1970s, with access from walkways at first-floor level, and with huge garages underneath. The bridges between walkways had soon been demolished, for they made it a muggers' paradise, and the garages had been barricaded as they had become a haven for arsonists. The way up to the flats was past rubbish-filled bins and up urine-soaked staircases. The area looked, and felt, threatening.

And the church building? Back then, it looked like a ruin in the heart of a jungle. The grounds were overgrown; trees grew from the roof; the windows of the former chancel were largely smashed, with rusting grilles hanging from them, enabling pigeons to fly freely in and out. Although Sunday worship still took place inside, locally the church was widely believed to be closed.

At my induction on 6 May 1998, the Secretary to the Parochial Church Council (PCC) expressed the hope that the church might be developed 'spiritually and materially, so that it may play a full part in the development and regeneration of our parish'.

So, has that been achieved?

The story

I first saw St John's, Angell Town on a windswept Saturday afternoon in October 1997. A long-standing member of St John's was a mourner at a funeral I had conducted that week. He told me that his vicar had died while on holiday in Ghana. My wife and I had come snooping. Straightaway I had a strong sense of a call to this place, despite the overwhelming air of dereliction that we saw – broken windows, tree-choked gutters, and flapping corrugated iron roofing. A damp sheet of paper was fixed with a solitary pin to a tree beside the church door: 'Father Michael's Memorial. Sunday 4 p.m.'.

A few weeks later we returned to meet the parish representatives, who would take part in the appointment process. The area bishop and archdeacon were encouraging me to think about coming to St John's as vicar. It was November. Rain was pouring down outside, and, as we ventured into the more remote recesses of the church building, rain was pouring down the inside too. Water deluged into overflowing buckets, in one room the ceiling was down, and pigeons fled as we came in. We felt as if we had stumbled into a Hitchcock movie.

It hadn't always been like that.

St John's is a typical mid-Victorian Gothic church. It was built in 1852, standing on the edge of Angell Town, then a new and prestigious private housing development. The architect was Benjamin Ferrey, a pupil of Pugin. It was listed Grade I and as a 'building at risk', and English Heritage were keen to see it preserved as a 'feature in the townscape' – that is, a remnant of the original Angell Town that had been largely demolished in the 1970s. The church was built with a tower at the west end, a nave, and a chancel at the east end, to which in the course of time some additional rooms had been added. Following a fire in 1947 the building had been divided, with the nave alone being kept for worship, while the east end had been converted into a community hall. In practice, this area proved impossible to heat and to maintain adequately. By the early 1980s it was falling into serious decay. Various attempts to find new uses for the space had come to nothing. The incumbent since 1972 had become increasingly ill and incapacitated, using a wheelchair for the last years of his life until his death, with the result that not only did the building decay but the congregation was reduced to a tiny faithful remnant.

My sense of a call to St John's was not diminished by any of this. On the contrary, a strong sense emerged that whatever gifts and skills I had developed over the years were appropriate to this situation. So it was that in the spring of 1998 I was instituted as vicar. The assumption that I and the members of the PCC made then, and probably never fully examined, was that the absolute first priority was to create a space fit for people to gather for worship.

Space for worship

Beginnings

In the months following my acceptance of the appointment, but before I became vicar, I felt that things were in such a demoralized state at St John's that I needed to attend PCC meetings and to do what I could to help with the building. I had preliminary discussions with the church architect in the hope that a detailed specification for emergency work could be prepared.

A major problem was lack of money. The PCC had very little in its own account and it owed the Diocese £9,000. Soon after I arrived, the Diocese generously wrote off that debt and offered a further £20,000 grant towards emergency repairs, with an additional loan facility. A small grant from the Church Urban Fund and another from a charity enabled some basic office equipment to be purchased. As a result, within a few weeks of my coming things were looking up. Pigeon mess was removed from the tower and the lavatory, high-level window panes in the worship space were replaced, and the pigeons that had taken up residence in the organ shortly before my institution were expelled.

Having access to some funds meant also that an electrical survey could be commissioned. The electrical contractor discovered arcing, pronounced the system an imminent fire risk, and promptly disconnected the heating and lighting systems. By the autumn it became obvious that worship in the church building was unsustainable without heat and light, particularly as the floor seemed to ooze condensation, forming a dank, mouldy slime. A generous offer from the church school to use their hall for Sunday worship during the winter months was gratefully accepted, and we worshipped in this school hall during the winter for the next four years.

Shortly after my institution I was approached by the BBC to use the vicarage, another Hitchcock-esque building, for filming. This produced further funds which proved invaluable later on when the congregation had to contribute its share of match funding.

A false start

Following a delay caused by the departure of the member of the architect's practice responsible for the work, a specification for essential work to the building was eventually submitted to English Heritage and the Diocesan Advisory Committee (DAC) in August 1998. In October I returned from holiday to find a letter from English Heritage saying that the report was insufficiently detailed and that 'we would not accept a further application for grant without a significant improvement in the quality of professional support'. This judgement was echoed by the DAC. The PCC decided to appoint a new architect and to ask the previous architect for his fee back. No response to letters was received, but thanks to the dogged persistence of the PCC Secretary, a large part of the fee was eventually recovered, after several delays, through the Small Claims Court.

This dragged on until June 2000. It was the first of many delays that seemed, at the time, interminable, and infinitely frustrating.

A new beginning

By December 1998 Thomas Ford and Partners had been appointed as architects. Early in the new year a fresh Quinquennial Report was complete, and by February a meeting had taken place with a quantity surveyor to look at items highlighted in the report. In May 1999 an application was submitted to English Heritage for grant funding towards emergency repairs costed at £250,000.

At last something appeared to be happening, and in order to underline the gravity of our situation, the decision was taken to remain worshipping in the school until the emergency repairs were complete. Little did we know how long that would take. Frustration got the better of us, and we returned to church as from July 1999. In the meantime, weekday festivals were celebrated with a Eucharist in the vicarage. Morning and Evening Prayer were said daily in the dank, dark, dismal surroundings of the church, to try to retain some sense that, despite appearances, this was sacred space.

Slow progress

Little was heard from English Heritage for many months following the submission of our application. Indeed, by December, English Heritage had still not submitted their report. I was researching charitable trusts and, in October, members of the DAC visited the site to consider plans for re-ordering the church. There were some helpful suggestions, and some bizarre ones, such as turning the worship space round by 180 degrees! (And where might that money come from?)

Our grant application ground its way through the English Heritage/Heritage Lottery Fund system. A grant offer was made in July 2000, which at least let us get on with approaching charitable trusts for further funding, but it presupposed an unrealistic level of fundraising locally. Our application for an increased grant was due to be considered at the end of January 2001, but that was postponed to a meeting at the end of February. Eventually, in March 2001, we were informed of a greatly increased grant offer, which meant that we only had to raise another £25,000. Thanks to the generosity of several charitable trusts, we achieved that.

And so a grant application submitted in May 1999 was finally agreed in March 2001. I am happy to report that since then English Heritage procedures have been somewhat streamlined.

Some extra financial help came, too, from letting the church building be used for filming. The downside was that during filming the *News of the World* somehow came across some posed photographs appearing to feature lesbian sex in the font (undoubtedly St John's font). These were published under the headline 'You Altar Be Ashamed!' There was a photograph of me looking clerically disapproving. Fortunately, I was booked on a plane to Mumbai the next day.

A sense of achievement

The faculty for the emergency works was granted in September, and building work finally began at the end of October. We had planned to move back into the church for its re-dedication when the Bishop of Southwark visited us in March 2002, but the building was not ready. More frustration. A service of re-dedication was finally held on 28 April. The worship space was watertight; it was heated, lit, and redecorated; a new tiled floor had been laid; the sanctuary had been extended and opened out; the brass eagle lectern had been stripped of its paint and polished; the font had been cleaned and repositioned. We had achieved a simple, light, open worship space, and we were very pleased and thankful. Many times, through the protracted months of delay, I had wondered if I had completely deluded myself about what God wanted in Angell Town.

And, more important than all the work on the building, despite all the disturbance caused by the demolition of the Angell Town Estate (of which more later) and the awkwardness of worshipping week by week in the school, we had a congregation back. Numbers coming to church had trebled in three years, and my own sense of vocation felt vindicated.

Space for community

But that sense of vocation was sorely tested by the other half of the project, for at the same time as developing the worship space we were trying to develop the nearly derelict east end of the building in a way that would benefit the community of Angell Town. The division of the building into two parts after the 1947 fire, and the urgent need to create a suitable base for the worshipping congregation, meant that we had little choice but to treat the two parts separately. The possibility of thinking about the building as a whole or, indeed, the entire church site including the vast vicarage, was never seriously addressed.

First thoughts

Soon after my arrival in the parish I visited a privately run nursery not far from the church. In an idle moment I read a table of the fees charged, which struck me as astronomical for local residents. I mused on the possibility of providing such a facility, charging fees that local people could afford. It did not take much research, back in 1998, to establish that there was no money available for that. It was an idea whose time had not yet come, and so it was set aside.

An apparently more productive way forward was to set up a small building development group, consisting of the church-wardens and other members of the PCC, and work towards raising the money to restore the east end of the building as a community centre. A consultation programme about potential use of the east end was carried out in early 1999 and a brainstorming session held with local community leaders and relevant local government officers. As a result we were able to prepare first a grant application to the Lottery Fund under the Poverty and Disadvantage Programme, and then a business plan. At the same time, a meeting was held with the Acting Community Work Adviser for the Diocese of Southwark. The grant application was never submitted. With no current use of the space, nor any likely potential user, we could not see how we could make a case for funding.

But then, in early 2000, through the good offices of the Brixton Town Centre Manager, we were put in touch with 198 Gallery, a local community arts project that was seeking larger premises. The gallery had an excellent record for fundraising. A series of meetings took place between gallery representatives and the PCC. For several months we had high hopes of a fruitful outcome. I met the gallery architect. Ideas of inserting a mezzanine floor were floated. And then nothing.

By the end of 2000 it was clear that the sums did not add up for the community arts proposal.

Desperation

In January 2001 a project appraisal meeting was called, chaired by the archdeacon, with representatives of all interested parties, including English Heritage, the PCC and the Diocese. We were able to demonstrate that we had exhausted the possibilities for a straight-forward community use of the building, and that there were great difficulties in obtaining funding for such use, when the only current users were pigeons. Among a number of options considered it was agreed that it might be necessary to think about conversion for housing, or some partial demolition.

Encouraged by the diocesan surveyor, who was keen to find a way of providing a new parsonage for St John's, another firm of architects was appointed to work on the development of the whole site. In the autumn, when work was beginning on the emergency repairs to the whole building, there came a moment of crisis. Proposals for the east end, which would have involved partial demolition, seemed to suggest a freeze on all work to that derelict area, whereas the continuation of the repair work, and the securing of grants for that, demanded that some emergency repairs to the east end be carried out. The suggestion from the church architects, Thomas Ford and Partners, that partial demolition could endanger the stability of the whole building, swayed opinion. The repair work was completed, and so the roof of the east end was now watertight. Radical proposals to alter the building were not meeting with favour.

A glimmer of hope?

At this point, in the autumn of 2001, I was invited to meet a member of Lambeth Early Years Development and Childcare Partnership, to be told of a possible source of money to create Neighbourhood Nurseries, administered through the local SureStart, a government programme aimed at providing a good start in life for children in their early years.

Through the spring of 2002, with support from the Diocesan Community Work Adviser, and the architect who had been working on the east end, a development group rapidly produced proposals to establish a Neighbourhood Nursery. This scheme also involved inserting a mezzanine floor so that office space for SureStart and a training suite for parents and childminders could be created. The nursery would be a partnership between the church and St John's School.

Although our proposals were not fully costed, and more work needed to be done on the design, we were confident that we had a viable plan, although it was difficult to obtain from SureStart consistent criteria by which our proposal would be assessed. It emerged that the available funding would be distributed through a competitive process, with three other projects from the local SureStart area. On 4 October 2004 all four projects had to make their presentation. We were unsuccessful and, despite involving the MP, could never obtain a full explanation for the rejection of our proposal. The successful proposal for our part of the SureStart area has in fact come to nothing.

Desperation, again

While work on the worship space had been completed, by early 2003 we seemed to have made no progress at all in the development of the east end. I produced a list of equally far-fetched options for the archdeacon, but we had no idea how to fund any of them. Number six was 'Padlock the b***** place and forget about it'.

But then it emerged that a substantial capital sum still remained earmarked for our project through the Neighbourhood Nurseries Initiative.

I had a telephone call from the Diocesan Urban Projects Officer to say that Christian Victory Group/I Care, who already ran a successful Neighbourhood Nursery in Stockwell, were looking for premises to open a second nursery, and that they already had some funding allocated to their project.

Were we interested? Were we!

Turnaround

Swiftly, representatives of church and school met representatives of Christian Victory Group/I Care and a three-way partnership was formed. The business plan was rapidly revamped. (Much time had been lost through the abortive submission through the local SureStart, and deadlines were pressing.) A successful application was submitted by the church to the (then) New Opportunities Fund for capital funding, while Christian Victory Group handled the application for revenue funding.

Under new plans, developed by Thomas Ford and Partners, the building was now to be handled quite conservatively, and so English Heritage/Heritage Lottery Fund money was available for the conservation elements of the project. (Try getting two lottery funds, with different target dates, to talk to one another.) All this enabled more money to be brought in from the London Development Agency, and from charitable trusts. A high point was our selection to be the South London project for the Bishop of Southwark's Lent Call. By June 2003 we even felt confident enough to invite the Archbishop of Canterbury to come and dedicate the project.

Building work started in May 2004 and was largely complete by the new year. The end of January 2005 saw the nursery project formally opened by the Mayor of Lambeth and dedicated by the archbishop.

But still no children were on site. A possible opening event after Easter was postponed because of additional requirements from OFSTED. At last, in September 2005, staff and children were in place, with numbers steadily growing towards the target of 49 affordable and quality childcare places.

An outcome

A building at risk has been saved; a blot on the landscape has been eradicated; a church in one of the most deprived parts of London has been provided with an income to use for future maintenance; parents, who could not otherwise afford childcare, are able to seek work, and their children have a delightful environment, providing them with stimulating experiences at a crucial stage of their development. Through many ups and downs, my very first thoughts about the use of the east end of St John's Church had borne fruit.

Reflection

Had we managed to develop the church 'spiritually and materially, so that it may play a full part in the development and regeneration of our parish'?

I don't know how spiritual development might be measured, but if numbers attending Sunday worship give any indication, then a three- or fourfold increase in the congregation since 1998 would suggest that the PCC secretary's hope is in the process of being realized.

Most of this chapter is about material development. A considerable transformation has been achieved. Yes, there are things we might have done differently. We might, for instance, have thought more about developing the site as a whole, rather than plunging into bringing the worship space back into use, but that is being wise after the event. We were led to a great extent by where funding was available, and we were constrained by being a listed building. Without the Grade II listing, demolition and redevelopment of the whole site would have been the only option.

But it is clear that the church has not yet played a 'full part in the development and regeneration of our parish'.

The project took place over years when the gruesome Angell Town Estate was largely pulled down and rebuilt, and what was not pulled down was extensively refurbished. I tried to take part in the Angell Town Partnership, which brought together local residents and the housing associations that were leading the building work. We invited representatives from the housing associations to some of our consultation meetings. It was half-hearted on both sides. With all the fundraising and negotiation for our project to do, I did not have the energy needed for the Partnership and there was no one else from the congregation to take a lead instead of me. I sensed from the local community that a derelict church building is the Church's responsibility, rather than an opportunity to create a resource to benefit the whole community. Maybe, too, there remains a sense that the Church of England is a white, middle-class outfit, even though the congregation of St John's is 98 per cent black, from a wide variety of backgrounds.

One effect of regeneration in the wider community has been to make the church congregation less local, and so perhaps less focused on its parish. To enable demolition to take place, people were 'decanted' to other areas. Many have stayed where they moved to, although they still come back to St John's to worship, increasing the sense that we are a Sunday-only church.

Since our return to regular worship in the church building, numbers attending on Sundays have remained at roughly the level they reached when we were worshipping in the school hall. On an ordinary Sunday the congregation consists of between 50 and 60 adults and 20 to 30 children. Many of the adults are in their thirties and forties and are of West African origin, although there remains a significant minority whose family roots are in the Caribbean. Sunday morning worship, a simple Parish Eucharist, remains the central focus of the life of St John's Church, but with virtually no activity beyond it. Development of church life is much constrained by people's work demands, over which they have no control, and equally strong family demands.

To a considerable extent the regeneration of the St John's building and congregation has been pursued in isolation from the regeneration taking place around it, so there are questions worth asking and reservations worth exploring about what has been done; but there remains a strong sense that we have achieved something really good, quite likely the best possible under the circumstances, and this increases people's sense of confidence and self-worth. We have a building that points to heaven and serves human need, and a building in which faith in God can grow and human dignity be affirmed.

10. Renewing the Culture

The Church on the South Bank

RICHARD TRUSS

The gates of Jerusalem will sing hymns of joy,
And all her houses will cry 'Hallelujah!' (Tobit 13.17)

William Blake, who lived on the borders of what is now Waterloo, had a vision of a tree filled with angels as he walked on Peckham Rye. This was one of those many spiritual encounters that transformed Blake into a prophet, poet, artist, oddball, and thorn in the flesh of his society. It was this illumination that enabled him to see clearly what most people wanted to avoid: the social exclusion of his day; and it was this vision that gave him an extraordinary hope that regeneration, and eventually the kingdom of God in England's green and pleasant land, was a real possibility.

In 2003 another angel came to St John's, Waterloo: the story of Tobias and the Angel from the book of Tobit, one of those books found in some Bibles between the Old and New Testaments. That year I met with David Lan, director of the Young Vic Theatre to discuss the possibility of a production of a new opera at St John's Waterloo, written by David and Jonathan Dove and based on the biblical story of Tobias and the Angel. David was keen that it should take place in a church building, a sacred space, but also a community space.

So it came to pass. A stage was built the length of the church with seating either side. The English Touring Opera and the Young Vic were engaged, and local people of all ages invited to participate. It showed that professional and amateur, trained and raw beginners, can successfully perform together.

The opera proved to be not only a week-long sell-out, but an unforgettable experience. Somehow in the evening, ordinary life embodied in Tobit, his dog and his family, and the people he encountered, were bathed in the beauty of heaven in the form of the angel and the sublime music. It was a performance that, to participants and audience alike, encapsulated the reality of regeneration.

The story of Waterloo's involvement with the arts goes back right to its beginnings when it was decided to develop this part of the south bank of the Thames into London's first industrial area. Even before that, it was home to Astley's Circus where Sergeant Major Philip Astley charged spectators a shilling to watch him do daredevil horseriding around a ring – the precursor of the modern circus. It was also the birthplace of the Music Hall, and most famously of all it was the home of the Old Vic Theatre, the only surviving building older than St John's Church. The link between theatre and church was to become very close. I have a picture of one of my predecessors on stage at the Old Vic, another was an actor in a previous existence, and today that link continues. Yet another of my predecessors turned the other church in the parish into a theatre, with regular productions, while St John's was used daily as a rehearsal space for the National Theatre, until it all proved too much for one of the churchwardens, who entered the church one day to find a motorbike being ridden at full tilt round the nave, and cast the whole company, Peter Hall included, out into the street. Such can be the ambivalence of our relationship with the theatre.

With the opening of the Festival Hall in 1951 and the subsequent developments of the South Bank Centre, the National Theatre, the National Film Theatre, the Hayward Gallery and the Young Vic, the parish of Waterloo has become a leading international centre for the arts. This has helped bring life to the South Bank and its hinterland, though it has taken years to turn Waterloo into the property agent's dream which it is now. For years, despite the prestigious arts venues, staff and audiences would scurry to Waterloo Station fearful of the inhabitants of Cardboard City or the rather threatening bleakness of the area.

The regeneration of the area has, as elsewhere, been primarily a development-driven phenomenon. Proximity to the City has made the area attractive, the major transport links, including in the last ten years those with the Continent, have increased this attractiveness, and the general trend for more people to move back into Central London, at least for a weekday 'pied à terre', has altered the whole character of the area. But it all exists cheek by jowl with what remains of the old Waterloo, with the council, Peabody and other estates, and with more recently built social housing.

Even in an area with so many prestigious cultural institutions in it, the arts can seem peripheral. They are there for those who like that kind of thing, or for outsiders. Certainly until recently few locals darkened the doors of the National Theatre or the Festival Hall. Genista Mackintosh, former executive director of the National, compared the theatre to the Church of England, with audiences of middle-class, middle-aged white people, the sort who were content to sit in rows and keep quiet for a couple of hours, who would depart after the show or the service with 'that was a good evening' or 'nice sermon, Vicar'. But of course all that has changed, both in the church in South London and in many ways in the theatre. Our churches are multi-ethnic, and the theatre and even the Festival Hall attract a real mixture of people, young and old, black and white. In particular, great attempts have been made to build bridges with the local community. If you are fortunate enough to live in the area, you will get concessions, sometimes free seats, and certainly a lot of encouragement to come along.

The relationship between the Church and culture has always been close. Churches have been patrons of the arts, have been musical centres, have, equally with the Greeks, given birth to theatre as we know it. Not that the relationship has always been comfortable. The vicar of St John's Drury Lane was deprived of his post at the end of the nineteenth century for visiting chorus girls backstage at Drury Lane. Today the Church's ministers are often chaplains to arts venues, and Waterloo's clergy have for some years been chaplains to the National Theatre. The Arts Centre Group, the Actors Church Union, the Catholic Stage Guild, and Arts and Christian Enquiry all promote this and other positive relationships between the Church and the arts.

But the arts have not been just something to be ministered to, but have also been an essential part of being the Church here. In this the church in Waterloo has had two advantages: the first is a large amount of physical space, and the second is the building's position at the centre of the Waterloo community.

Creative St John's

St John's has the great advantage that it is a large Georgian box, built originally to seat 2,000 people, but was bombed in the war, in one blow removing the side galleries and fixed pews – something that would have taken years of negotiation with the Diocesan Advisory Committee and English Heritage to attain in peacetime.

Underneath was a Crypt that for many years was home to the North Lambeth Day Centre, ministering to homeless people in the area. There was also the newly rebuilt St Andrew's Church just 400 yards to the south in a predominantly residential area. Recently the Day Centre closed after essential funding was withdrawn. This produced a dilemma and an opportunity. The dilemma was that as a church that had sought, at one remove admittedly, to meet the needs of the street homeless, we were no longer doing that, and yet home-lessness still remained a very visible local issue even though actual numbers had reduced considerably. The opportunity was the availability of the Crypt and the new St Andrew's as a place for new initiatives.

Here the danger was that we just filled them with anyone who wanted to come along, especially if they would pay for it! Churches quickly end up hosting a random set of activities with little or no coherence, and often with no clear link with the church itself and its role. We become simply managing agents of buildings. It may help to pay our contribution to diocesan funds, but it has no clear link to our raison d'être.

We gradually realized that what was needed was first some over-all vision, and we approached this in what may appear an odd fashion. We called a Saturday meeting of the Church Council and looked at how we might 'brand our church', almost like a commer-cial company might brand a product. What were we trying to say about the church and its relationship to the wider parish? What words or ideas linked what was already going on in the life of the church and its buildings with the wider community and would make sense to both? Top of the list came 'Creative'. Everyone was very aware that Waterloo, particularly the South Bank, was a creative centre. They knew as well that many people felt excluded from that. They were aware too that there were already many creative activities going on in the church itself and that this had been the case for many years. Above all, God's creativity and re-creativity were at the heart of what we specifically had to offer as a church.

The next question was how to build on all this. We already had a long history of use of the church by theatre groups, orchestras, and exhibitors. It was our bread and butter, and in terms of Christian mission it was justified largely in terms that if people came into our building, something of the gospel 'just might rub off'. As far as I know, this often-made claim by churches has never been properly analysed. It might equally be that people attending a concert at St John's might come away with the impression that it had become an arts venue rather than a church. Certainly the situation lacked any real coherence, any sense of being part of a thought-out strategy, or of having a relationship with the worshipping congregation (most would be totally oblivious to what went on in church from Monday to Saturday), or with the local community.

That is not to say that everything was like this. We had hosted a successful series of art classes by the Dulwich Picture Gallery during which the church itself had been filled with a wide spread of local people, including one or two who had been sleeping on the church steps, and who wanted to try their hand with the brush or palette knife for the first time since they had left school. We had run lunchtime concerts for residents and local workers. Local schools, artists and organizations had put on exhibitions. Yet there was something piecemeal about all this, and its relationship to the core activity of the church remained unclear and by and large unconsidered.

St John's Crypt

With the Crypt becoming available and the completion of the new St Andrew's, it was the moment for putting a 'Creative Vision' into practice. We had strong links with two arts organizations who were already using church facilities and with whom we had a good rapport. Together with them we decided that we would form a partnership to run what we called the 'Creative Crypt'. We have since been joined by another organization, so there are now four parties to the partnership. In the future there may be more.

We agreed that we would be a partnership of equals and that no decisions on the use of the Crypt or anything related to it would be made without the consent of all. This involved the church giving up some of its power, but the advantages are already proving well worth any loss of authority. First it means that the load of financial responsibility is spread, and in particular future fundraising for maintenance and improvements can be shared. Of course, from a technical and legal point of view, the Parochial Church Council (PCC) remains the final arbiter and is where the buck stops, but practical devolution, with the church as partner rather than landlord, creates a sense of common ownership and purpose. All the partners are enthusiastic about how the Crypt is to be used and improved and about how to share the common areas, down to what to put on the walls and what brand of coffee is served in the kitchen.

All the users have to be arts-related. At the moment the four are: an orchestra for young musicians, a mosaic project working with young offenders and local youth clubs, a theatre company which works with school-refusers, and the church. Each has its own relationship to the wider Waterloo community and to one another. So, for instance, the orchestra works in local schools but also offers free concerts in the church; and the Mosaic project undertakes projects in public spaces in Waterloo, including the churchyard, and welcomes members of the church youth club to its studio. All of the projects meet over a cup of tea in the common space in the Crypt. Eventually we hope there may be joint activities and real interaction.

In this way, the whole is becoming greater than the parts, and all would quite happily see themselves as part of the church through being 'Creative St John's'. In one way the church is just a partner, in another it is something of which they and we are all part. We are learning something of practical inclusivity.

St Andrew's, Short Street

In addition to St John's, there is a brand-new church building in the parish: St Andrew's, Short Street. It replaces two former buildings, one destroyed in the war, and the second a 1950s crematorium-style church. This was a substantial building, with a church, two large halls, offices and a peal of six bells. It was realized some time ago that it had outlived its usefulness as a building, was expensive to maintain, and had no particular architectural merit. It was finally, to everyone's relief, demolished in 2002.

In its place there is now a brand-new, smaller, though still substantial, church, paid for from the proceeds of flats being built on part of the site. Similar developments have taken place all over the UK with varying degrees of success. One of the advantages of being in central London is that property values have soared, so the sale of flats has financed a well-designed building using some of the best materials available. We, like all others who have been through such a process, have realized that this is a once-and-for-all opportunity. This poses a major question for the churches. In rationalizing our plant and selling property, are we squandering the resources of the future?

The new church has a worship space on the ground floor seating up to 80 people. Above it there are three further floors with proper lift access. One includes a large area available for youth work and community events, and on the others there are offices and meeting rooms available for the parish and the wider community.

St Andrew's will have its own life and its own individuality, but at the same time we have recognized that what goes on there must complement and work with what is taking place at St John's. It too comes under the 'Creative' umbrella. This is being realized already in the use of space by local theatres and other arts bodies, in the forms of worship on Sundays and weekdays, and in the fabric of the building itself. There are stained-glass windows designed by Victoria Rance, with undulations of light from floor to ceiling in the worship area, in the upstairs hall and in panels on the main stairs. She has also created a sculpture representing a fishing boat and net for St Andrew, and a beautiful metalwork font that stands in the tiny outside garden. These have all transformed what could be a pleasant but utilitarian building into a place where you experience real spiritual beauty.

In some ways it seems very odd indeed to build a new church in central London, which many would say was already over-endowed with churches. However, one of the positive things of the last few years has been the revivification and repopulation of the inner city. The latest census figures have shown that the population of the parish of Waterloo all but doubled between 1991 and 2001. Our own community work has also grown. But above all we felt it vital that St Andrew's was still there in the heart of a distinct area of the parish. To withdraw, however much financial sense it might have made, would have been a damaging message to the local inhabitants. A church building can speak loudly of the presence of God, and in our case we hope that it speaks too of the creative God who brings new life.

St John's churchyard

Another area that has brought surprising links and creativity has been the churchyard. Like all older churches, St John's had an extensive burial ground round the church. This was cleared of gravestones through the initiative of Octavia Hill, the great Victorian housing pioneer and co-founder of the National Trust. She had the vision of the churchyard as a place for the living as well as the dead. It was planted and turfed and a children's playground incorporated, the first of many such cleared churchyards in London.

Over the years it deteriorated and became a scruffy space mainly frequented by the local hard drinkers. Most local people and workers gave it a wide berth. But now things have changed and, largely due to a continuing initiative led by St Mungo's, the homelessness charity, the Waterloo Green Trust, Lambeth Council and the church, the space is being reclaimed. First, a new memorial garden was formed, including a wall plaque designed by students from Central St Martin's College with a few lines of William Blake printed on it. Soon after, a knot garden was planted on the south side of the church and it has now become an annual tradition for the congregation to walk round this garden during the main Eucharist on Easter morning. Finally, we are looking at the main grassed area. A day-long consultation was held to air three suggestions for this space – a Japanese Peace Garden, an educational space, or a Sculpture Garden. Opinions were more or less evenly divided, but the narrow favourite was the Sculpture Garden.

The design and use of this space will be important. It will need to accommodate a variety of sculptures, permanent and temporary. It will provide an opportunity for local artists to exhibit and a space for visitors and regular users of the churchyard to enjoy works of art. From the church's point of view, it will be important to link what is there outside the church walls with what is going on inside. Possible ways in which this might happen would be to have displays that are linked, or to have a church stall outside or some form of open-air worship, or occasionally to provide music in the open air that links with a musical event within the church itself.

As with the buildings, the overall aim is to see it all holistically. What goes on in the church buildings needs to link with what goes on in the churchyard, and also needs to link with the wider community. It is so easy to work in a piecemeal fashion with little sense of overall purpose.

Strangely, perhaps, one of our main aims has been to ensure that the church remains at the heart, and is seen to be at the heart, of all that goes on – not to claim it for the church in a proprietorial sense, but to see it all together. Here our branding exercise continues to pay off. The litmus test for any proposed use of any space is whether it contributes to creativity. Church, churchyard, Crypt, and St Andrew's up the road, are to work together as one.

Secular or sacred?

The relationship between the Church and the arts has been an ambivalent one. On the one hand, the Church has been a patron and in some cases – such as the theatre – a place of origin for the arts. On the other hand, the Church has seen much done in the name of art as a threat – or even sometimes as of the devil.

A friend recently spelt out what he saw as the essence of art – he was particularly thinking of the theatre, but what he said could apply to almost any art form:

- It expresses what it means to be human.
- It reconnects people with their own innate creativity.
- It helps people to rediscover play.
- It reconciles people.
- It articulates both the joys and sorrows of the human psyche.
- It allows the quasi-ritualistic enactment of what cannot be spoken.
- It can subvert demagogues and give society a voice.

If all this is true, you might say that the Church had a natural ally in

the arts, or even conversely that it might be put out of business by
the arts. Not for nothing has Tate Modern been called the cathedral
for the twenty-first century. But the Church comes in as the one
responsible for naming the presence of God and articulating the
gospel. The way we allow others to work with us in our church
buildings will be an important part of this. First of all the buildings
themselves have to continue to be clearly places of worship and
prayer. Nobody should come into St John's Church, whether it be for
a concert, a play, or an exhibition, without knowing immediately it
is a working church. That does not mean that there will be a prayer
at the beginning from the vicar, or any other overt religious statement, but that the building should be clearly a place for daily worship. So, like it or not, anyone in the audience will make connections
between the church and the concert they are enjoying. Though the
music may be the same, it is not the same as going to the Festival
Hall.

The same applies to our working with people from different arts
organizations, such as we now have in our Crypt. Whether they be
individually Christians or not, they know that they are part of a
working church where the Church's agenda is paramount; and at
the same time they will be affirmed in what they are doing themselves. It is proving important here that we in the Church are not
seen as landlords or distinct from them, but that we are partners
with them. Here the Church can be a true servant, perhaps offering
something as simple as tea and biscuits; or the clergy can be chaplains to the organizations, 'being there' for people, or inviting people
to lunchtime prayers or to a study group.

Sometimes the arts events themselves will be overtly Christian, as
with a performance of the St John Passion or a play based on the Acts
of the Apostles. Sometimes they will be part and parcel of worship.
Therefore we have used our links with local arts groups, and the
talents of members of the congregation can bear fruit too. We have
been privileged to have a director of the Young Vic put our young
people through their paces for a small drama for Sunday worship.
We have also been treated every year to a carol service led by a choir
that uses the church. At another act of worship in which I was
involved, students from the Royal Ballet School interpreted the
theme of the readings in dance. For most performances there will be
no such obvious link, but that doesn't mean that they are separate
from the church.

The arts and religion are not in separate camps. The traditional
gulf between sacred and secular is not what it seems. So much of
what is called secular art has a sacred purpose if we mean by that
that it reveals something of God to us. On the other hand, some of

what is looked on as sacred really reveals nothing of God because it is just plain bad art.

One of our tasks at St John's is to do all we can to abolish that artificial barrier between what is regarded as sacred and what is seen as secular or profane. God is to be found in it all. Art should be about what Peter Brook calls the Invisible-Made-Visible, and for us that must mean the divine. The Church's work is to be interwoven both with that of those who use its buildings and with the wider community – and that work includes acknowledging the creative and redeeming work of God.

A few years ago, Marianne Faithfull agreed to give a concert in St John's in aid of our work among the homeless. She stood in the chancel and performed a programme of songs from Kurt Weill. Tickets were sold and a number were given by a generous benefactor to members of the homeless community resident on the steps of the church and the Waterloo Bullring. They came in force and mostly sat in the gallery and proceeded to heckle the introductory speakers and Marianne Faithfull herself, to the extent that she stopped a song, put two fingers up to the gallery and suggested that they 'F*** off!' The Bishop, MP, Mayor and other guests were remarkably sanguine and unflustered by all this. The concert continued, with occasional interruptions mainly from Barney, an elderly alcoholic who was intent on discovering his skills on the organ, and from fights breaking out intermittently in the lobby.

In one way the whole evening had been a fiasco and had no obvious relation to the task of the church, other than raising some money for our homelessness charity. But it is still remembered with affection by all those who came, including, I hope, Marianne Faithfull herself. The church was venue to a concert and was still the church, and the audience had included all sorts of people, many being brought together for the first time in their lives. It was holy chaos, but through it there was a sense of fun, of shock, of the posing of questions, of lives being touched, of vibrancy, and of God.

Further reading

Brook, P., *The Empty Space*, Penguin Books, Harmondsworth, 1968.

Gorringe, T. J., *Furthering Humanity: A Theology of Culture*, Ashgate, Aldershot, 2004.

Morisy, A., *Journeying Out: A New Approach to Christian Mission*, Continuum (Morehouse), London, 2004.

11. Starting from Scratch

The Greenwich Peninsula

MALCOLM TORRY

> Great is the LORD and greatly to be praised
> in the city of our God.
> His holy mountain, beautiful in elevation,
> is the joy of all the earth,
> Mount Zion, in the far north,
> the city of the great King.
> Within its citadels God
> has shown himself a sure defence. (Psalm 48.1–3)

When I arrived in the Parish of East Greenwich in 1996 most of the Greenwich Peninsula was a desolate place. On the western side, alongside the Blackwall Tunnel approach road, was Tunnel Refineries, a food refinery (now owned by Tate and Lyle, but with fewer employees, though still producing sugars and starch from wheat), Alcatel (which used to make submarine cables and now repairs them), a chemical distribution depot, and a deep water terminal and aggregates yard. But on the larger eastern side, where there had once been Europe's largest gasworks, all that remained was one gasometer (still working), a small engineering company (on a site that had once been occupied by a parish church, St Andrew's), two pubs, an old school (now a theatre scenery store), a site occupied during the winter months by a group of travelling circus-workers, and a lot of poisoned land.

The Millennium Dome

Then came the Millennium Dome: a highly successful exhibition to celebrate the millennium. The press rubbished it, but members of the chaplains' team knew otherwise. The Dome received more visitors than any other visitor attraction in the country during 2000; approval ratings were high; and we often met people who had returned for their third or fourth visit. Schoolchildren had an enjoy-able and educational day out, and the staff were well motivated and well trained, and several major companies arrived to recruit them as the end of the year approached. And part of the success story was the chaplains' team: about 20 of us, all volunteers, and drawn from a variety of churches. Our task was to be available to staff and employees, to hold a brief service of Christian prayer twice a day in the Prayer Space, and to make the Prayer Space available to a variety of different faiths for private prayer and for the celebration of their major festivals. Relationships between the different faiths were good, and particularly with the imam who visited regularly.

Then, on the last day of the year, the Dome closed. The chaplaincy team held a celebration lunch, we gave a Peter Kent painting of the peninsula to Nicholas Rothon, the Roman Catholic priest who had co-ordinated the chaplains' team, and said goodbye to one another. But I didn't say goodbye to the Dome, for while the Dome was closed to the public there were still people there: security guards, maintenance staff, and the drivers of machinery demolishing the exhibition. English Partnerships, the government's regeneration agency, charged with taking care of the site and finding a future use for it, was happy for a chaplain to remain, so once a month I walked the now familiar route from Westcombe Park to the end of the peninsula to pass through the empty corridors of the once-busy service building and on to the site. For a while the canteen remained open, but that too then closed, and, after the equipment auction, the place emptied and my monthly visits took half an hour at most.

Meridian Delta Limited's development

After the government had spent two years failing to find a viable future use for the Dome, English Partnerships sought a developer for the entire eastern side of the peninsula. The land had been cleaned before the Dome was built, and already the Millennium Village was slowly taking shape to the south of the peninsula (John Prescott handed over the keys of the first home at the very end of 2000). It was eventually realized that to invite submissions of masterplans for the whole of the peninsula north of the Village might be the best way to realize the area's potential. It was, and it is.

Meridian Delta Limited (MDL) was declared the preferred bidder: a consortium comprising Lend Lease (an Australian transnational corporation) and Quintain Estates and Development plc (which owns some land on the north-western corner of the peninsula). MDL and English Partnerships, together with Anschutz Entertainment

Group (AEG), an American entertainment company (best known recently for producing *Narnia* and who have responsibility for redeveloping The O2: the new name of the Millennium Dome), were granted planning permission by the London Borough of Greenwich in February 2004.

In 1999, long before MDL's masterplan, Greenwich Borough had prepared a model to show what they thought the peninsula might one day look like. It was housed in the Greenwich Pavilion, which had been built to the north of the Dome, on the tip of the peninsula, to house Greenwich's exhibition, a 3D cinema, and a café. Some visitors to the Dome found the Greenwich Pavilion, others didn't – but those who *did* find it discovered within it a history of the peninsula and a model of what it might look like one day: all covered in housing.

The model wasn't entirely accurate. The food refinery is still viable, and, unless prices in the sugar market make production on the peninsula unprofitable, it will continue to be so. But most of the peninsula will be densely built housing, mainly flats around large courtyards. Most of this housing will be owner-occupied, and it will be expensive; but some of it will be social housing, managed by a housing association; and some of it will be shared ownership, enabling key workers such as nurses and teachers to buy part of a property and rent the rest.

The kind of people who will live in the new development isn't entirely predictable, but the population of those parts of the Greenwich Millennium Village already built might give us some clue as to who might choose to live in the homes soon to be built on the rest of the peninsula. In the owner-occupied properties there are lots of young couples without children; there are young couples with one or two young children who are looking for somewhere else with a garden; there are gay couples of all ages; there are employees of banks and other city institutions staying for a few weeks or a few days in flats owned by their employers; there are students and groups of young adults in flats that other people have bought in order to rent them out; in the housing managed by Moat, a housing association, there are families of all shapes and sizes; and in the owner-occupied property there is the occasional family who love the idea of the ecology park which is on the site, and approve of the ecologically friendly policies of Greenwich Millennium Village, and have moved there because of these.

It wouldn't be surprising if we saw the same mix in the new housing to be built north of the Village. This means that it might be a struggle to ensure that enough children, teenagers and elderly people live on the peninsula (for a balanced community needs them). It is very helpful that there is already a primary school in the

Village, and that the John Roan School, a nearby secondary school, is to be rebuilt on the peninsula.

But the new community on the peninsula won't just be residents, for as well as the new homes there will be office and retail space, the schools, the health centre (already built in the Millennium Village), Ravensbourne College of Design and Communications (a higher education corporation that is relocating from Chislehurst), and, of course, The O2.

In the summer of 2005 the builders moved into the empty space inside The O2 to start to build a huge entertainment district for Anschutz Entertainment Group. There will be a 23,000-capacity arena for music and sports, and around it a street with clubs, bars and restaurants on either side, along with cinemas, a theatre, and an exhibition space (Tutankhamun is coming in November 2007 for the final leg of its worldwide tour before returning to Cairo). If the government agrees, there will be a regional casino; and outside the Dome, on the northern tip of the peninsula, where the Greenwich Pavilion now stands, there will be a new luxury hotel. The plans wouldn't look out of place in a sci-fi film.

All this will take 15 years to build, and by the time it's finished there will be 24,000 residents, 24,000 employees and 24,000 visitors on the peninsula every day. A sizeable and very diverse new community. And to this community the faith communities have a contribution to make.

The beginning of a relationship

As soon as MDL were appointed I rang them up – for the Greenwich Peninsula is in the parish that I serve, and to relate to major developments in the parish is one of the Team Rector's responsibilities. It took a little while to get past the PR company MDL had appointed to manage relationships with the press, but before long I was talking to Susie Wilson, appointed by MDL to manage all of its relationships with the communities around the peninsula. Knowing that such an appointment had been made was in itself a considerable encouragement, and Susie and I were soon discussing how the faith communities in Greenwich could relate most constructively to the new development. The Greenwich Multi-faith Forum (a forum that representatives of the borough's different faith groups attend), the ecumenical borough deans (each denomination in a borough appoints a representative to forge relationships with the civic authorities), the South London Industrial Mission, the Archdeacon of Lewisham, local churches, and a variety of other people were also discussing the same question, so the obvious thing to do was to hold a meeting, which we did in March 2003.

It was already clear that MDL and the borough council wanted the faith communities to work together in the new community planned for the peninsula. MDL's commitment to such working together was to a large extent inspired by their experience of Bluewater, the large retail destination near Dartford, which Lend Lease had built. There they had installed a Prayer Space for the use of all the faiths and, while recognizing that the peninsula development was really rather different, they wanted to replicate that experience as far as possible. Another very practical reason for asking the faith communities to work together was that the masterplan envisaged high densities and no land left over for other organizations to build stand-alone buildings. This meant that if there was to be space for congregations to gather then it would have to be a single space, and the obvious solution, quickly agreed, was that the Greenwich Pavilion would be rebuilt on the eastern edge of the peninsula and would be used by the faith communities for worship, prayer, education and community development.

It might also be a struggle initially to generate a sense of community in such a large new housing development in which many residents are working long hours in the city, spend their leisure time all over London, and go away at the weekend. The faith communities clearly have a role here, in the same way as the churches did during the massive expansion of South London's suburbs during the 1920s. During that period the Bishop of Southwark, Cyril Garbett, raised funds for the erection of new church buildings and for the extension of existing ones.[1] The new populations arriving on the large housing estates in Downham, Mottingham and elsewhere found church buildings already there, and thus opportunities to gather as well as places for prayer. Congregations, and the buildings in which they meet, have always made new community activity possible: a process that continues today.

But it is now 80 years later, and faith communities in the Borough of Greenwich are not just Christian. The new community on the peninsula will not be just Christian either, and we expect residents, employees and visitors to be of a wide variety of faiths. The offer of the Greenwich Pavilion on a site in the midst of the new development represents the borough council's and the developer's recognition that the faith communities will want to serve this new community together, and that by doing so they will make a large contribution to the sense of community that will develop on the peninsula. It is also a recognition that one of the important functions that the faith communities can fulfil is the linking of the new community to the existing community of East Greenwich. If you walk from the terraced streets and local authority estates of East Greenwich towards the peninsula, then one of two major inter-changes underneath the tunnel approach road, or one of two long footbridges, has to be negotiated. And then initially all you find is industry, a retail park, or derelict open space. There is a serious physical barrier between East Greenwich and the community on the peninsula. Part of our task will be to ensure that there is less of a psychological barrier than there might otherwise be.

The outcome of the meeting was an agreement that the faith communities would work together, that we would also use the Greenwich Pavilion together, that we would treat our relationship with the development as a single evolving project, that I would co-ordinate the faith communities' relationship with the new development, and (at my request) that a steering group would be established to which I would be accountable.

The appointment of a single individual to relate the faith com-munities to the development has been interesting. Even though they might appear to be centralized bureaucracies, multinational corporations are in fact highly decentralized, and the local manager of a particular project is expected to take decisions. Of course, large decisions require discussion, and might require decisions to be made elsewhere; but it is still the case that important decisions are frequently made locally, and that they are made quickly. While the same isn't quite so true of local authorities, there is now much more of a culture of individual cabinet members taking decisions, and of officers taking decisions on the basis of agreed policy. This suggests that if a long-term relationship between a developer, a borough council and the faith communities is to succeed, then individuals are going to need to relate to individuals, and those individuals are going to need to be trusted to take decisions. Sometimes decisions will need to be consulted on – but timescales will be short and decisions, once taken, will need to stay taken.

So far relationships between the developer, the borough council and the faith communities on the Greenwich Peninsula have been very positive, and an important reason for this is that the steering group to which I'm accountable is made up of committed people from a variety of faiths: a Muslim, a Jew, a Baha'i, a Sikh, an agnostic, and several Christians of different denominations. The steering group is now a charitable trust, the Greenwich Peninsula Chaplaincy Steering Group, so its members are trustees and respon-sible for the activity of the chaplaincy: and at each meeting I report to the steering group, we review progress, we make plans, and we decide on policy.

Chaplains to construction workers

As the first stage of the development is a large construction site in and around The O2, the chaplaincy's first task was to set up a team of chaplains to serve construction workers. With much help from Susie Wilson and Sir Robert McAlpine (the main contractor), three of us started work as volunteer chaplains in April 2005, and five more were recruited the following autumn. Greenwich Local Labour and Business (GLLaB: established by Greenwich Council to enable contractors to recruit workers locally) most helpfully organized the necessary safety training for chaplains, and from March 2006 a team of eight chaplains has been operating on the site from Monday to Friday. Every day, for a couple of hours, a chaplain is on the site. We might spend time in the two canteens, or wander round The O2, or visit the offices. We are available to listen, and the better known we become, the more the workers talk to us. Every now and then we meet. This is difficult to organize, as we are all volunteers and getting everyone together is a nightmare; but it is essential to share concerns that have been raised during conversations (anonymously, of course); and a handful of issues have subsequently been discussed with the site's management.

The chaplains' team is almost as diverse as the steering group: a Muslim, a Sikh, and six Christians of different traditions.

Working as a chaplain on the construction site, and with this group of chaplains, has been a real pleasure. The whole world is here – not just among the chaplains, but on the site as well. There are construction workers from the Indian subcontinent, Africa, Latin America, Australia, New Zealand, the USA, Canada, Singapore, the rest of Europe (and especially Poland and the Czech Republic), and almost everywhere else. Conversations are about the work they are doing, their families, their faith, the meaning of life, their plans, politics, football (in which I don't even pretend an interest: there's no point) . . . and then there are the difficult conversations: the racist ones, the ones full of prejudice of one sort or another, and the ones about other people on the site. We listen. Sometimes we say things that need to be said, each in our own style.

And as we do this work we are always aware that we represent not ourselves, but the communities of faith to which we belong. To help us to do that the steering group has established a Council of Reference to enable us to stay closely in touch with the leaders of our communities. Each faith community represented in the borough is invited to send people to the council's meetings, which are chaired by Christine Hardman (Archdeacon of Lewisham, for the Church of England) and Richard Moth (vicar general of the Roman Catholic

Archdiocese of Southwark). Numbers fluctuate, but it's a useful way to make sure that communication channels remain open. It is important that the Steering Group is independent of every particular faith community, and it is equally important that we don't abuse that independence – for we work on behalf of the faith communities in this particular place. The Council of Reference is a means of checking out that we're not going off on a tangent along which local Muslims, Jews, Sikhs, Hindus, Buddhists, Baha'is and Christians are unlikely to want to follow us. Another way of ensuring this is regular reports to Greenwich's Multi-faith Forum (the secretary of which is Saeed Ahmad, one of our trustees); and it is through the Multi-Faith Forum that some of our chaplains have been recruited.

At each stage of the project we have tried to learn from the other chaplaincy models that we have come across. For example, in the early days we visited the Prayer Room at Canary Wharf (where different religious traditions gather at different times for worship); we visited a multi-faith centre in Kilburn (which helped us to decide on a 'level playing field model', in which the different faith communities are equal partners constitutionally, rather than a 'host and hosted' model), and both Steering Group members and chaplains have been much helped by visits to Bluewater where the longstanding chaplain, Malcolm Cooper, and his team of volunteer chaplains, have shared much wisdom with us. We have also invited people to join us at Steering Group meetings: people with expertise in employment law, community development, and different kinds of chaplaincy; and representatives of Anschutz Entertainment Group, Kerzner International (the casino and hotel partner in The O2), MDL, and the Forum@Greenwich (a centre for integrated living also involved in community development: the Forum will be one of our partners as we do community development together in the new community).

The next steps

In the summer of 2007 The O2 will open, and our next task will be as chaplains to the arena and the surrounding entertainment district. This will all be much more like our chaplaincy work in the Dome during 2000 than like our work on the construction site – and we are of course taking advice on how to undertake this kind of chaplaincy. I've been a chaplain in a hospital, a theatre, the civil service, a food refinery, a police station, a banana distribution depot and a construction site. Whether any of this is adequate preparation for chaplaincy in a night-club is an interesting question.

Some of our experienced construction site chaplains will be needed on the new construction sites that will open next year for the building of residential property, and then the new school, the college, the 'Millennium Square' (the working title of the new main square between North Greenwich underground station and The O2), the hotel, and finally the office accommodation. We shall therefore soon be recruiting new chaplains for the entertainment district, and again we shall be looking for chaplains from a variety of faiths and with a diversity of experience. And again we shall be using the Greenwich Multi-faith Forum to recruit them, along with other networks as we find them.

A casino?

By the time this book is published we shall know whether Greenwich has been awarded the one licence available for a regional casino.

In 2005 the Steering Group held its own discussion on gambling and casinos in preparation for the inevitable public debate on the possibility of a casino opening on the peninsula. We agreed a paper and circulated it as our contribution to the discussion.

As the Gambling Bill progressed through Parliament the Methodist Church and the Salvation Army commented in detail and at length. They welcomed new regulations designed to remove slot machines from shops where they can easily be accessed by children, but were less happy with the idea of regional casinos able to install hundreds of machines with 'variable stakes and prizes', as they are surely right to believe that an increase in problem-gambling will be the result. There is some relief that there won't be slots for credit cards on these machines. The Church of England and other religious bodies have expressed their agreement with the Methodists' and Salvation Army's approach.

As the Bill progressed, forty regional casinos became eight, and then eight became one, which meant that where there had been almost complete certainty that AEG would be opening a casino on the Greenwich Peninsula, there was now anything but.

And then in August 2006 I was invited by the government's Casino Advisory Panel (CAP) to the Examination in Public of Greenwich Borough's bid for the one regional casino licence on offer. Someone asked me whether I knew that the CAP's website contained a letter that looked as if it was from the chaplaincy and supportive of a regional casino on the peninsula. Had we written it? No, we hadn't. I e-mailed a complaint, I received an immediate e-mailed apology from AEG, and I thought that the matter was closed. But then someone leaked the e-mails, the *Daily Mail* put me on its front page, and four television news crews arrived on the vicarage doorstep. My consistent message was that the paper on the CAP's website was a not very good attempt at summarizing our 2005 paper, that they'd forgotten to clear it with us, and that I didn't regard the mistake as malicious, which I didn't.

(It isn't usual to reprint lengthy documents in books of this nature, but given the importance that our July 2005 paper has now assumed, I think that it's worth breaking the rule just this once – so this document is reprinted as an appendix to this chapter.)

In the paper we tried to say two things at once: first, some of our religious traditions are totally opposed to gambling and some take a more relaxed attitude, but because a new high-stake regional casino might turn *potential* problem-gamblers into *actual* problem-gamblers, who will damage themselves and people around them, none of us was in favour of a regional casino coming to the Greenwich Peninsula; second, if a casino were to be built in The O2 then we would regard the pastoral care of employees and visitors as one of our tasks.

Here is an example of the diverse roles that faith communities need to take on in today's plural society: the proclamation of the wisdom contained in our traditions, critique of projects proposed by government and transnational corporations, care for the vulnerable, and continued involvement in the institutions of our society. Being chaplains to a casino, knowing that there are arguments for it being there and arguments for it not being there, being on the side of those who think it *shouldn't* be there, but understanding those who take a different position – this is the complexity that faces any chaplain in any institution, but perhaps in a more acute fashion in a casino than in many other places. The casino focuses many of the characteristics of our life today. It is therefore essential that we should be involved, and essential that we should be involved together. It might be that Christians will benefit from the clarity to be found on such issues in the sacred writings of other religious traditions, for, as one member of the Steering Group said: 'The Bible doesn't help us much here.' It might also be that other traditions will benefit from the debate between Christians on such issues. Perhaps as we do some work together in a casino on the peninsula we shall understand more clearly the relevance to this issue of what the Bible does say on a whole variety of possibly related issues; and perhaps by doing this work we shall test whether it really is possible to keep pastoral ministry and prophetic ministry together.

As I write, we await the CAP's recommendation as to where they

think the one regional casino should be located, and after that we
shall await the Secretary of State's decision.

And then?

There will be 10,000 new homes, enough office space to fill two and
a half Canary Wharf towers, a sky-reaching hotel, the college, the
school, the shops. To enable us to relate to all of this there will be the
Greenwich Pavilion: the green steel and glass building currently
surrounded by high wooden fencing, but that will be relocated to a
small open area on the riverfront halfway down the peninsula.

In this building the faith communities will worship separately.
We are a *multi*-faith chaplaincy, not an *inter*-faith one: that is, we are
doing together what all of us in good conscience can do together,
and not doing together those things that we can't all in good
conscience agree to do together. This means that worship will be
separate, though in the same space – so, as in the Prayer Space in the
Millennium Dome during 2000, if a congregation requires objects to
help it to worship, then these will be brought in at the beginning of
the event and removed again at the end. (I can foresee a little
difficulty over storage, but I'm sure we'll manage.) And no doubt
the different faith communities will undertake their own distinctive
education and other related activities. But there will be things that
we can and shall do together: learning about one another's faiths,
social events, availability, hospitality, continuing chaplaincy to
The O2 and other institutions on the peninsula, and community
development. That is, we, with our partners, shall do all we can to
promote the health of the new community on the peninsula – not
just of each of its members, but also of the community as a whole.

As for the Church of England, its particular role will be the
establishment of a congregation or congregations on Sunday and at
other times, in consultation with other denominations and other
faiths (and the Steering Group has already created a draft weekly
timetable for the Pavilion; it's better to do this well in advance so that
each faith community can do its planning according to its own
timescale). But it isn't the 'Church of England' that will do this,
of course. It will be the Parish of East Greenwich with help from
neighbouring parishes. Already the Parochial Church Council has
committed itself to supporting a new congregation, and when plans
for the Greenwich Pavilion have been finalized, more detailed
planning will take place. Initially, of course, it will need people from
existing congregations to get it going, so that there's something for
new residents to join in. And then it will become theirs, and a third

district of the parish will be established alongside the existing districts of East Greenwich and Westcombe Park. What will be provided will be distinctively Anglican. It will have to be – because that's our contribution to the diverse whole. In the same way, Roman Catholic worship will be Roman Catholic worship, Free Church worship will be distinctively Free Church, Friday Prayers will be precisely that, and Jews, Sikhs and Hindus, and perhaps other faith traditions, will do what is distinctive to themselves. By this means we shall all be true to the revelation that we have received, and we shall have that revelation to offer to the new community.

As the community grows, congregations, chaplaincy and community development will be our contribution to community-building, and during the next 20 years we shall see an evolving, diverse relationship between the faith communities and an evolving, diverse community.

Regeneration

So, what lessons have we learnt?

First of all, what have we learnt about regeneration?

We have learnt that good communication is essential – and we are very fortunate that LendLease is the major active partner in this development, that they arrived intent on consulting locally, and that Susie Wilson has done it well. And we are fortunate that AEG is also able to enter into dialogue with the local community, and that whatever the difficulties we have all experienced in relation to Greenwich Borough's bid for a regional casino, we are all still talking to one another and planning together for the future benefit of the new community on the Greenwich Peninsula.

We have learnt that there are always more questions than answers. What will it be like living in mixed-tenure housing, with the different tenures mixed up together? What will it be like living in some of the densest housing in the UK? What will it be like to have over 20,000 residents, over 20,000 employees and over 20,000 visitors on this patch of land every day? Can a casino bring 'regeneration'? Will people be willing to do without cars (and about one-third of the residents will have to)?

We have learnt that catching a vision together – the borough, the developer, the community and faith communities catching a vision together – is a good basis for conversation about the character of the development and about much else besides.

And we have learnt that the faith communities can work together in new developments like this one.

The Greenwich Peninsula development is the largest single regeneration project in London. Every regeneration project is different, so we can't read off from one project what might be useful in another – but it might be that the ways in which the faith communities have related to this development contain lessons for elsewhere. One of the lessons that we have learnt is that clarity about motives isn't always possible and that maybe that doesn't matter. What matters is that we aim to serve the new community, that we aim to do it together, that we consult widely as we do it, and that we adjust our approach in the light of changing circumstances and of our listening to others.

Why is it that the faith communities are working together on the peninsula? Because MDL want us to? Because the borough council wants us to? Because we want to? Because if the different faith communities argue for their own individual buildings they might not get any, but if we work together we shall have a building to use together? Because this is the way of the future and we happen to find ourselves doing it this way sooner rather than later?

Why is there a single individual through whom all communication travels? Because it's more convenient for MDL, the borough council, the contractors? Because it's a statement that the faith communities wish to work together? Or because none of us can face the complexity and delays that working with the normal decision-making mechanisms in faith communities would subject us to?

Why have we established a Steering Group as an independent charitable trust? In order to relate more easily to MDL and the borough council? In order to be able to plan coherently? Or in order to keep it all out of the hands of particular faith communities so that we don't have to cope with constant negotiations about everything?

Probably 'yes' to all of those.

We have made mistakes, and I'm sure that we shall make some more. Our mistakes as well as our successes will have lessons to teach to others involved in regeneration projects; and our discussions about whether some incident is a mistake or a success might contain even more important lessons from which others can learn.

And maybe something else that we are learning is that we only understand the Church's role in regeneration projects when we're in the midst of trying to make such a relationship happen. It is only by getting on with it that we understand how to do it. Action first, then consultation, then reflection, then different action. Is not this how God's Spirit leads us into truth? In a society as complex and changing as ours, we simply don't have the luxury of being able to consult at length, decide what to do, and then do it. Yes, we must do a certain amount of that – but only, I would suggest, in the midst of the activity. What matters is making relationships, doing some work, taking difficult decisions, keeping channels of communication open, doing new things, and doing different things at the same time: the prophetic and the pastoral, the separate and the together, worship and chaplaincy, prayer and community-building.

And finally, how can the Church of England enable this kind of work to happen? By ensuring that any large regeneration project is in a single parish or by establishing a conventional district (Canary Wharf was not in a single parish and no conventional district was formed, and we've learnt from that experience); by its clergy staying long enough to see large parts of a project happen (which can mean being there some time before it starts as well as being there while it's going on); by providing the necessary resources (both human and financial: difficult in a cash-strapped Church, but essential nevertheless); and by housing clergy in new developments (the Diocese of Southwark is soon to sell the vicarage in Westcombe Park and create a new one on the peninsula: an imaginative project over which MDL's designers and the diocesan surveyor are co-operating).

Above all, the Church at every level needs to encourage experiment, for every regeneration project is different from every other and in each place the Church will need to do it differently.

Further reading/websites

www.greenwich-peninsula-chaplaincy.org.uk
www.meridiandeltaltd.com
www.theo2.co.uk
www.greenwich.gov.uk
www.aegworldwide.com
www.englishpartnerships.co.uk
www.culture.gov.uk/cap/

Notes

1 Cranfield, N., 'Art and the Sacred Space: Art and Architecture in the Parish', in Torry, M. (ed.), *The Parish*, Canterbury Press, Norwich, 2004, pp. 100ff.

Appendix

The Greenwich Peninsula Chaplaincy Steering Group's paper on the proposed casino, July 2005

Anschutz Entertainment Group, one of the members of the Meridian Delta Ltd. consortium, is building a 20,000 seat stadium inside the Millennium Dome, and Kerzner International has been discussing with Anschutz the possibility of opening a casino next to the stadium. If the number of regional casinos permitted by the Gaming Act rises, then several large casinos of the type envisaged will be built in various parts of the country, and the Greenwich Peninsula, with its good communications both locally and nationally, is clearly a desirable site. If the Government gave permission for such a casino inside the dome, and Greenwich Borough gave it permission, then it would be built.

The Greenwich Peninsula Chaplaincy Steering Group, and particularly its Council of Reference, represents the current and future involvement of the faith communities on the Peninsula. It must therefore speak for the faith communities on this issue and also make clear its own position.

Our religious traditions lie along a spectrum. They all discourage their adherents from gambling, but some have a more permissive attitude than others. The Qur'an forbids gambling to Muslims: 'O you who believe! Strong drink, games of chance, idols, and divining arrows are an infamy of Satan's handiwork. Leave it aside so that you might succeed' (5:90). The Hindu Scriptures forbid gambling to Hindus: 'Oh man! Do not gamble. Cultivate your cornfield. Enjoy that gain and deem wealth so acquired as enough' (reg ved 5:85:8); and so does Baha'u'llah, the founder of the Baha'i faith: 'Gambling and the use of opium have been forbidden unto you. Eschew them both, O people, and be not of those who transgress' (The Kitab-i-Aqdas, p. 75, 155). Similarly a code of Sikh conduct and conventions, based on the Sri Guru Granth Sahib's discouragement of gambling, tells Sikhs not to 'steal, form dubious associations, or engage in gambling'. For Judaism and Christianity gambling, whilst not specifically forbidden, must be seen in the light of such important principles as love for one's neighbour (Leviticus 19:18; Mark 12:31) (for a gambler's gains are someone else's losses) and the responsibility to care for one's family (Ephesians 5:25ff) and for children. Children are a gift (Genesis 33:5) and a blessing (Psalm 127:3), and they need particular care (Matthew 18:1ff).

Whether gambling is forbidden or simply discouraged, this is often for a practical reason: 'that you might succeed': and this is where the agreement lies between the faiths, for they all recognise that gambling can prevent human flourishing and that it should therefore be avoided. So in the Sikh Scriptures, 'the gambler's consciousness is focused on gambling' (Sri Guru Granth Sahib, page 1180, line 7); and a Buddhist text, *Digha Nikaya*, reads: 'There are these six evil consequences in indulging in gambling: the winner begets hate, the loser grieves for lost wealth, wealth is lost, the gambler's word is not relied upon in a court of law, he is despised by his friends and associates, and he is not sought after for matrimony, for people would say he is a gambler and not fit to look after a wife.'

The Methodist Church and the Salvation Army commented in detail and at length during the consultation on the Government's Gaming Bill. They have welcomed new regulations designed to remove slot machines from shops where they can easily be accessed by children, but are less happy with the idea of regional casinos able to install hundreds of machines with 'variable stakes and prizes', as they are surely right to believe that an increase in problem gambling will be the result. There is some relief that there won't be slots for credit cards on these machines. The Church of England and other religious bodies have expressed their agreement with the Methodists' and Salvation Army's approach.

We live in a plural society and a secular democracy, and any Government must legislate for what it sees as the common good (which will not necessarily be that envisaged by any particular religious tradition), must preserve individuals' freedoms (sometimes even if someone's exercise of those freedoms might damage themselves and others), and must often choose between a variety of evils. The Government might argue that there are increasing opportunities to gamble in other countries and on the internet, and that it is sensible to try to keep gambling in this country where it can be both regulated and taxed. And Greenwich Borough might argue that if one of a number of large regional casinos isn't built in this borough then one will surely be built somewhere else in London, some other community will reap any economic benefit which might accrue, and residents of Greenwich will still be likely to gamble there. We might not agree with these arguments, but we recognise that they might be made.

In such a context the faith communities' task is to speak for the vulnerable: for people tempted to gamble, and for their families – for by doing this we love our neighbour. And here speaking for the vulnerable means pressing Kerzner to provide spaces in their casino where there is no gambling, where there are comfortable seats, and where there is someone to listen; it means ourselves providing care for those people who are having difficulties with a gambling obsession; it means services for families suffering from problem gambling – and all of this requires a positive relationship with Kerzner, Anschutz Entertainment Group, and the London Borough of Greenwich. Such a positive, communicative relationship is what we intend.

And in such a context it is also our task to continue to speak the wisdom contained in our Scriptures and the wisdom which has evolved in our respective traditions.

We believe that these two tasks are compatible with each other.

12. Congregations Are Mission

Building Congregations in Thamesmead

JEDIDAH ENOCH-ONCHERE AND
SIMON BOXALL

What should be done then, my friends? When you come together, each one has a hymn, a lesson, a revelation, a tongue, or an interpretation. Let all things be done for building up. (1 Corinthians 14.26)

In *Great Expectations*, Pip met the convict, who we discover later on is his father, on the marshes round Thamesmead. The infamy of the area was further developed when Stanley Kubrick filmed *The Clockwork Orange* in the toddler stage of growth of the new town. Now, we have a McDonalds and a KFC. It makes you wonder who is in charge of publicity for Thamesmead!

One thing you can be sure of about Thamesmead, it's big – so big in fact that a previous vicar of one of the churches in the area (William Temple) recently revisited and got lost. People still sometimes refer to the area in which we live as 'the Thamesmead Estate', and there are places with just rows and rows of houses with no centres to draw the residents together and act as catalysts for community-building. Thus Thamesmead can feel pretty anonymous. However, almost since the building began in a wave of optimism in the 1960s, the Church has been fulfilling its role of salt and light, not always with the comfort of the local authorities as its primary consideration. Those who have been around a long time still speak of people such as Thamesmead clergy Jim Thompson and Patrick Forbes with great affection. Through the work that they did, the Church was noticed and seen to be involved in the community.

So, just how was, and is, the Church involved in the community? What we would like to do is to give you a brief history of the area, with the 'smelly bits' left in. Jedidah will then illustrate the Church's (both Anglican and wider) involvement in that. West

Thamesmead's recent growth and the beginning of the Open Gateway Church will then be described by Simon.

For our Thamesmead town, the optimism began with a grand regeneration design, which was thought visionary for a new town in close proximity to the east end of London. The Greater London Council (GLC) planned a modern and enjoyable place to live in, and architectural scholars came to marvel at plans for this new creation. The generous numbers of parks, lakes, waterways and below-the-surface walkways gave Thamesmead the features of an expansive park.

When responsibility for housing was taken away from the GLC, it was time to rethink how the town's regeneration would be managed, and in 1986 the town's management was handed over to Thamesmead Town Ltd, a private company run by residents. It was to be the first time in the capital that a private company would be given such a responsibility. The question was: how would the housing portfolio be efficiently managed and the grounds maintained to cope with the high rate of the town's growth? In May 2000, with further growth on the horizon, Thamesmead Town Ltd was divided into three separate segments: Gallions Housing Association Ltd, Trust Thamesmead Ltd (Community Development and Care) and Tilfen Limited (Commercial Development). They function independently.

All three segments have thrived. Gallions Housing Association owns and manages approximately 5,000 units of which 10 per cent are leasehold, 131 are shared ownership, and 60 are retail units. It also owns parklands, waterways and lakes. The Gallions group now consists of Gallions Housing Association, Thamesmead Landscape and Tilfen Land Ltd, and the group is playing an active role in the Thames Gateway regeneration. New developments include a retail park, Gallions Reach Ecopark for sustainable homes, and £2.7 million has been secured for mixed-use development with homes, retail and office facilities, and a hotel, at Tripcock Point to the west of Thamesmead.

Trust Thamesmead has provided the much needed community support, especially in training and capacity building. It also inherited seven community halls, mostly managed locally by residents' committees.

As regeneration was taking shape, plans for improving educational standards got underway. In September 2002, the first City Academy opened its doors to tackle the under-achievement in Thamesmead and the surrounding areas. Our celebrated Business Academy Bexley, which now dominates the horizon next to the concrete housing blocks, replaced Thamesmead Community College and was a result of public and private partnership funding. In its first year, it provided 1,350 places for 11–18-year-olds. This number is set to increase.

The Ecumenical Project

Jedidah Enoch-Onchere

I arrived in Thamesmead from Milton Keynes in 1998. Within six months of my arrival, I was co-opted on to St Paul's Parochial Church Council (PCC). The PCC had representation from the United congregation (Anglicans, United Reformed Church and Methodists), the parish team ministry and Roman Catholics. I came to realize that, unlike my former church in Milton Keynes, St Paul's Church buildings and its community resources were intended for sharing. To formalize the sharing, the Thamesmead Ecumenical Partnership Project Agreement had been signed over 20 years previously. It provides for the Anglican, Roman Catholic, Methodist and United Reformed Churches jointly owning St Paul's Church and the Church of the Cross: and the St Paul's Church building was divided into two spaces (one for a United Congregation made up of Anglicans, Methodists and members of the United Reformed Church, and one for Roman Catholics) which could be combined to enable the two congregations to worship together. The aim was for the churches to provide leadership in the community and to demonstrate cohesion and integration. Indeed, in the late 1990s, the then Anglican team rector, Canon Chris Byers, played a leading role in the long and complex consultation process that created the new Trust Thamesmead. St Paul's was the only large venue next to the town centre and therefore doubled as a hall for social functions. Ironically, while the discos drew in teenagers to full capacity on Saturday evenings, only a handful of worshippers attended Sunday services. In 2001, after several attempts, Chris Byers's successor finally convinced the PCC that some of the teenage activities that went on in the United Congregation worship space were contrary to our Christian teaching. The use of St Paul's for discos ceased forthwith.

While Canon Chris Byers led a strong church presence in the social and economic functions of the town, the ambitious ecumenical project was ailing as members struggled to celebrate a common faith while retaining denominational identity and traditions. A new team rector, the Revd Barry Thorley, brought a new sense of the importance of a congregation gathering for worship. The problems were that so much energy was being expended on joint decision-making, that clergy of different denominations rotating around the churches meant there was too little consistent pastoral care, and that nationally and globally the hopes generated by the Second Vatican Council and the Anglican–Methodist discussions had led nowhere. This had left the monthly joint Roman Catholic, Anglican and Free Church worship at St Paul's as an isolated demonstration of disunity rather than as the short-term experiment that it was intended to be.

The solution was to abandon the monthly Roman Catholic, Anglican and Free Church joint worship, to retain Anglican–Free Church joint congregations at both St Paul's and the Church of the Cross, and to locate Free Church ministry at the Church of the Cross and Anglican ministry at St Paul's.

Building numbers was now more important for the United Congregation. I remember one Sunday morning in 2001 when the new team rector, the Revd Barry Thorley, courageously preached that there was strength in numbers and went on to challenge the congregation to invite more members to fellowship with us. But first he encouraged us to brighten up our chapel, making it more inviting to newcomers in Thamesmead. A dozen volunteers painted the church, added a few furnishings, and transformed the space.

Immediately the mission to build congregations gained momentum. For all clergy, serving a congregation and serving the community are important, but for different clergy the balance varies. For years a strong leadership for the town's regeneration was accompanied by a diminished Sunday congregation of 40 or under. With a new team rector, the focus shifted on to growing the congregation, and St Paul's now experiences one of the highest Sunday attendances in the Diocese of Southwark. The increased numbers confirmed that there were people in the community whose needs were yet to be met. So the question was: 'Where should we lay our emphasis, inside or outside our churches?' We formed a core group to pray and seek solutions. There were no simple answers, but two issues were brought to light. First, that it was important to be flexible and to embrace change in order to reach people outside the church doors. (We've done this together in West Thamesmead; see below). Second, that it was unrealistic to expect our priests to perform all functions successfully. Therefore it was necessary to increase lay leadership so that the maximum amount of community and spiritual leadership could be provided. From the turn of the century, we have grown two ordained non-stipendiary ministers, one still in training, a licensed reader and three people enrolled on the Bishop's Certificate course. These members joined the core group that helped to build our congregations.

There were areas of worship that needed to change. New parents were bringing in one-month-old infants for initial welcoming and prayers, and families kept the church informed of counselling and prayer needs in the community. This was the beginning of the growing of our new congregations. The Spirit was starting to move. The number of children increased from five to over sixty. There was a need for a junior church that would cater for the different ages, and for a youth group. In order to meet the needs of a community, spiritual needs have to be met, and this we were doing.

It quickly became apparent that most newcomers saw the Church of England as an institution with boundless resources for supporting its churches and members. They also expected the priest to be available at all times, the junior church to run every Sunday, the church to be clean and warm, and the music to sound like that of cathedral choirs. It came as a surprise to some that the machinery that runs the church derives energy from within the congregation, and that financial support for the parish needs to come from the congregation. One of the most difficult activities of our church was running stewardship campaigns and getting people to give regularly. Perhaps humility prohibited us from asking.

St Paul's adopted ways of worship that are more appealing to Thamesmead's newcomers, mainly of African origin. The congregation has Praise and Worship sessions when they sing, clap and beat drums. If these new ways of worship attracted new members, they isolated the older white members. Some chose to worship elsewhere or to move to midweek services. They made it clear that they felt alienated and were unwilling to accept change. In a similar manner, the lack of modern gospel music and intensive Bible study haemorrhaged our teenagers to Evangelical and Pentecostal churches. These are two examples, but many more are found in our community where integration is still difficult to achieve.

There are many reasons why families attend church. In some cases, because of cultural and social change, we seem to have lost our traditional values founded on God's Word in the Bible. Such loss hinders integration and increases suspicion of, and resistance to, new cultures. Young families turn back to religious observance in order to protect traditional values which help them to endure the harsh changes happening in our society. They want to shield children from the social ills prevalent in the inner cities.

Of the families of African and Asian origin, a fair percentage attend church. This churchgoing population is easy to bring in through our church doors without invitation. The bulk of the remaining work to be done is with the white population who are secularized and self-confessed agnostics, atheists or spiritualists. We know that some do not participate not because they do not believe, but because they do not see any point in doing so. People from other ethnic backgrounds live in Thamesmead, especially the southern part, but remarkably there does not seem to be a very strong presence of other faiths in the area. That is not to say that they do not exist, only that they have few adherents.

Thamesmead is a town with a strong Christian presence. It was said that one street in Thamesmead has no fewer than six neighbouring households, well known to each other, and each growing its own new church. We have yet to witness the strength of these churches truly uniting to transform the town of Thamesmead even more.

Christians Together

Christians in Thamesmead and Abbey Wood had worked well together in the community for over three decades. In 1999 the Diocese of Southwark seconded the Revd Chris Beales to the team ministry, partly to help organize Millennium celebrations. At the first meeting that he convened it was resolved to form an informal grouping of the local churches in Thamesmead and Abbey Wood Estate, the Christian Community Partnership (CCP). The CCP aimed to take the opportunity afforded by the Millennium Year for some joint work by the churches in the wider community. The churches and congregations taking part included the Anglican, Roman Catholic, Methodist and United Reformed Churches (partners in the long-established Ecumenical Partnership), and also the Baptist, independent and black-led Churches. As the numbers of churchgoers was small at the time, it made sense that they should share services and facilities. It was certainly never conceived that there would be increased rivalry in recruiting from a small pool of those that were willing to attend church. A large sector of the population was secularized, a fact that forced churches into aggressive recruitment of 'floating' members during the Millennium year. As it happened, the floating members were the ones embracing ecumenism or sharing and they were uncomfortable with the compartmentalization that came with full membership of churches.

I retired from the CCP in favour of my successor as churchwarden. It still meets once a month to arrange common activities, for example carol services, Easter celebrations and summer festivals. Back in 1999, the CCP identified priorities that included building a family centre and a community hall, the idea being to create a facility for a 'one-stop shop' in Thamesmead offering a range of services under one umbrella, including counselling and support, information and advice on welfare benefits and social security, crèche and child-minding facilities. These same ideas were already being discussed at PCC meetings soon after I joined. They were not realized, and priorities have changed along the way. In any case, the Law Centre at St Paul's and other organizations provided most of these services. But one of the notable outputs of the CCP was back in November 2000, when it produced an audit report that quantified and put value to services, resources and facilities available in Thamesmead and Abbey Wood. This document, updated and extended, will be useful to our Open Gateway Church in West Thamesmead.

The Open Gateway Church: Mission in West Thamesmead

Simon Boxall

By the beginning of the twenty-first century, Thamesmead was looking a bit more settled – but a new stage of growth was about to begin. And begin it did! Houses and flats started to appear at an astonishing rate. Would they be blots on the landscape, or flowers in the desert? The Diocese of Southwark knew that it had to play its part in trying to ensure that the growth would turn out to be more like flowers than blots. Plans were therefore made to bring a member of the clergy to live and work in West Thamesmead. A vicarage was built, a support team was put together, people continued to pray . . . and in January 2005 my wife, Rachel, and I arrived from Brazil. The task? To build a church in West Thamesmead, an area of about 15,000 people and still growing.

Where do you start? It's a blank canvas, and I was always better at painting by numbers. We began well, by spending time praying and settling in, and that process continues. We should then, perhaps, have tried to formulate a clear vision of what we wanted to see happening and have an idea of what sort of picture we wanted to create on the canvas. But we didn't. We accepted, of course, the support of the other members of the ecumenical team, and then we just started trying out different things. We knew that a church only exists if there are members, which is hardly rocket science. We did not have the challenges, or the advantages, of a church building, so the vicarage became the centre of our activities. The Portuguese word *congregar* means to draw together, and that is what we have been trying to do. Through contacts that we were given, and an old-fashioned leaflet drop, a group of six, then seven, then nine people began to meet on Sunday evenings for a time of worship, prayer and Bible Study, with occasional Home Communions.

The way forward that seemed to be indicated was to concentrate on building up that small and fragile congregation. That has been done by undertaking an Alpha course, and by growing. Using the talents and responding to the needs of those around us, three other small groups have been established, two Craft Clubs, and a Coffee Morning which caters mainly for mothers and toddlers. Although there is nothing overtly 'Christian' about any of these gatherings, the needs that are mentioned in conversation are included in prayer when we meet on a Sunday.

The fact that we have a decent-sized garden has meant that we have been able to hold several barbecues, which have drawn in a good number of people, about 35, and these occasions have been used to invite those who know little about the Church to find out more. We are very happy that the vicarage is used so much as we have always felt that the house in which we live should be open to all. People are free to pop in whenever they wish, for a drink, a chat, or a prayer. There is no other immediate gathering place for this to happen. There is a small 'Village Hall' at the other end of West Thamesmead, but it is not well sited to serve those who live in the newest houses. For now, the work here has to focus on the creation of many small cells or congregations. The support of the other churches in the team, Church of the Cross, William Temple Church and St Paul's Church, is therefore all the more important as their existence gives our groups the opportunity to meet up with them in larger gatherings. There has also been tremendous support from the Diocese through the Diocesan Missioners, the Community Development Officer, and the Bishop of Woolwich. Suggestions have been made and acted upon that have resulted in the Open Gateway Church becoming relatively well known in the area. The fact that there are others around is a great incentive to make sure that days are not filled with building castles in the air.

Earlier I mentioned that we didn't formulate a clear vision of what we wanted to do in West Thamesmead. We just had the vague sort of notion: 'plant a church'. What did we mean? Who would do it? We had been throwing paint at the blank canvas in an apparently haphazard way. Over time, and we believe that this was definitely guided by God and to some extent despite us, a picture has in fact begun to appear. Although our vision in itself is still very much a work in progress, I believe that it is becoming clearer all the time and will guide us more and more over the coming weeks, months and years. The Open Gateway Church sees itself as 'a group of ordinary people being transformed by the love of God into extraordinary people, who want to share that love with those around them'.

Are we seeing changes? So far we have not seen dramatic transformations, but people's lives have been deeply touched in 'ordinary' ways. Take Christina for instance. She first came to us as a result of the leaflet that had been pushed through her letterbox. She and her neighbour, who has had contact with the Church in the past, turned up for one of our Sunday times of worship, and stayed, initially because she felt welcome. She was at that time in an unhappy relationship with her partner, but was staying with him at least partly because of their daughter. As the weeks went by she began to open up more and ask prayer for various topics. She later said how 'spooky' it was the way that these prayers were being answered, and she was not shy about telling others unconnected with the church about this. When we ran the first Alpha course, she participated eagerly and was surprised that nobody seemed to find her questions or comments 'stupid'. Soon after the course she was confirmed by the Bishop of Woolwich. I wish that I could say that after this everything became rosy – but it didn't. What did happen was that she found the strength to leave her partner (by mutual agreement their daughter went with her), and overcome the bureaucracy that surrounds the receiving of housing benefits. During this time of struggle she found the support given to her by those connected to one or other of the Open Gateway 'congregations' enabled her to live one day at a time. Now she is engaged to be married (yes, she is a little embarrassed by how quickly this has happened), and her fiancé is keen to participate in the next Alpha course that we will be running.

The other person who was confirmed with Christina was Dave who had spent some time in prison. Because of his prison sentence and his age, he has not been able to get a particularly good job. He has also had various problems with his health. Despite all this, his growing faith is transmitted to others by his cheerfulness and his caring attitude. He is married to Kay who has a sister who suffers from agoraphobia. With Kay's loving encouragement – some might call it friendly bullying – she began to come to the Craft Club 'congregation'. Through that, she has found the courage to go out more and more, and even appear at one of our barbecues.

During the writing of this chapter I had a minor heart attack in Cumbria and was unable to get back to Thamesmead for nearly a month. The empowering work of God, however, enabled the small group in West Thamesmead to keep going and to keep reaching out to others.

None of these stories is particularly dramatic, but they do point to the way in which we are trying to be or 'do' Church in this part of Thamesmead. In God's strength we want to see more lives transformed, and we want to see the area in which we live become a community, with the Church at its centre. Contacts have been made with Trust Thamesmead and Gallions Housing Association, as well as with a nearby Neighbourhood Watch scheme. It may be that as a result of these contacts a building will be made available where many more community and church activities can take place.

The Wider Community

Jedidah Enoch-Onchere and Simon Boxall

Responses to the needs of the community exist in all of the churches in our parish. These are channelled through weekly newsletters, devotional materials, ministries of reconciliation, confession, training and prayers for healing. Joint pilgrimages and retreats are commonplace. To enrich these activities, the church runs a women's group and a crèche, makes home visits, organizes visits to Belmarsh Prison and old people's homes, offers legal advice, and puts on a range of young people's activities. Some of the life-changing experiences of this work are witnessed in the Open Gateway Church that we have shared above.

Each of our churches provides a range of activities. For example, St Paul's houses the Law Centre that provides a wide range of legal advice, debt counselling and welfare benefits advice. Weight Watchers used to meet weekly and Kelly's dancing uses the premises.

Our church at William Temple Church offers ministries of reconciliation and confession and support. There is a pre-school group and crèche, and 'Heart in Art' runs an Arts and Crafts group with people with mental health problems. But the programme with the most community impact is Neutral Ground, which provides children whose parents live apart with the opportunity to spend time with the parent they don't live with in a supervised and supportive environment. Between 35 and 40 children and their parents attend each Saturday.

The Church of the Cross has a playgroup and a youth club for 11–18-year-olds that organizes aikido classes as well as dance and drama. The church is one of the venues for the CCP children's holiday club during the summer holidays. Also for the wider community, there is one-to-one support for people suffering from HIV/AIDS and a food store for people urgently needing provisions. The Methodist minister, the Revd Gordon Newton, is also a chaplain at Belmarsh Prison and at the Greenwich and Bexley Cottage Hospice.

One of the District Church Council members once said that 'the growth of our mission in Thamesmead reflects that of a newly born baby. The high peaks of Christian activities are prompted by an event.' This rings true especially when we look back and recognize that the first event was the creation of the ecumenical experiment, which excited members into sharing and serving the one God. Then it went into slumber mode until the racial killing of young Ronan Adams just before the murder of Stephen Lawrence. This resulted in the Rainbow Days, which targeted the inclusion of young people and encouraged racial harmony. In the same spirit, the schools were encouraged to participate in the Brownies and Scouts activities. Beyond mere participation, the church school, Bishop Robinson School, produced designs for stained-glass windows in our church. These were contributions by a group of young people who have made lasting connections with the church.

All of our efforts in growing our mission have revolved around housing and its diversity. Much of the earlier stock was classified as social housing, and the older blocks of flats, singularly unattractive to look at, have many problems related to inner-city deprivation. Thamesmead still has many social setbacks. Youth gangs, high unemployment among young black males, substance misuse, exclusion, depression, teenage pregnancies and environmental degradation are some of the urgent issues that the community needs to deal with.

Even though we have welcomed the newer housing, and especially the attractive new housing in West and Central Thamesmead, it now proves to be too small to accommodate a family with older teenagers or for people whose cultural inclination is to share their home with parents or relatives.

The strength of Thamesmead lies in the good mix of a growing number of young people. We have ethnic groups and cultural diversity: white, black African, black Caribbean, Chinese, Vietnamese, Asians, and a growing number of people from Eastern and Central Europe. Unlike some other London townships, the town is managing change without some of the desperate racial and other tensions of the past. The relative calm possibly arose from teaching people tolerance. Each person is made in God's image. Therefore we are the same before God, and this equality transcends all perceptions of superiority. Hopefully, this message is slowly filtering into the community.

The church here in Thamesmead has 'Great Expectations' for the future. No doubt there will also be Great Frustrations, but, whatever happens, the Thamesmead United Parish is in this for the long term, seeking to be transformed by God's love, and aiming to see this part of London being transformed from an ordinary suburb into an extraordinary one.

Further reading

Beales, C., *The Churches in Thamesmead – Their Presence, Interests, Involvement and Influence in the Town*, Christian Community Partnership, London, 2001.

Housing Corporation, *Housing Corporation Assessment Report: Gallions Housing Association (L4274)*, Housing Corporation, London, July 2003.

Wigfall, V. G., *Thamesmead: Back to the Future – A Social History of Thamesmead*, Greenwich Community College Press, London, 1997.

13. Lots to Do

Project Development

SUE HUTSON

Have you not heard? The LORD is the everlasting God, the Creator of the ends of the earth. He does not faint or grow weary; his understanding is unsearchable. He gives power to the faint, and strengthens the powerless. Even youths will faint and be weary, and the young will fall exhausted; but those who wait for the LORD shall renew their strength, they shall mount up with wings like eagles, they shall run and not be weary, they shall walk and not faint. (Isaiah 40.28–31)

We want to do something . . . it's daft having our churches and buildings closed for several days a week . . . there is so much happening in our area now and we just don't know how to join in . . . our faith inspires us to serve the community, but how can we do this with the buildings we've got? . . . actually I'm not sure I understand the new language that is being spoken in my community about regeneration . . . I have not got time for pointless meetings, but I want to do something for the community in which I live.

Above are just some of the questions and comments that I bump into most days in my work for the Diocese of Southwark as parish churches explore their vision and mission, begin to research project ideas, or develop their existing work in their communities.

As communities are influenced by the massive regeneration industry, the church and its associated activities may often be the only dependable constant, with a history in the area, that is committed to 'the involvement of all sections of the community, including marginalized groups'.[1]

Regeneration cuts deep into people's everyday lives, and for those churches that minister to communities where change and development are taking place, being the Church alongside the people who live and work in such areas brings both opportunities and challenges. It is encouraging to see that this issue is being engaged with from a number of perspectives. In 2004 *Mission-shaped Church* hit the bookshops. It invites the Church of England to consider crossing cultural boundaries in its mission. This was then followed by the *Faithful Cities* report, in the spring of 2006. This celebrates and challenges the ways in which churches are working, and highlights a number of key factors for consideration when thinking about and working around the subject of regeneration. This chapter will not repeat what can be read elsewhere, and I won't seek to unpack the issues around regeneration, and whose agenda it comes under and how local communities can be winners or losers in the developments, or the wide-ranging impacts that occur. This chapter contains some basic steps that you may want to consider when thinking about a community project, and an exploration of how these steps work out in practice.

Aptly, this chapter's title is 'Lots to Do' – for this is so. But don't be put off, because you will find that the processes you are going through are not only informative but are also exciting and fruitful experiences. You can't jump from having an idea to seeing it all happen, no matter how well intentioned that idea might be. There are stages that any community project needs to go through in order to ensure that it works efficiently and effectively and for the benefit of all concerned.

Vision seems an obvious place to start, yet so many community-related projects can miss out this part of the process when considering a community project. Your vision is going to be the vital foundation stone of all that you will undertake as you develop your project, and it is the 'touching place' that ensures that all parties are working to the same end. It can be a guide and a guard which confirms you are on the right track. It is your vision that is going to turn into a reality, so it's worth investing in this at the beginning. A vision should be something that is energizing and carries the commitment and enthusiasm of your team. A vision should be something that you can articulate clearly and is share-able, and it should be something that is realistic but also builds on gifts, experiences, aspirations and calling.

A vision may begin to take shape because you are discerning something new happening in your church, because the community around you is asking for something, because you have identified a need, or because you have recognized a problem in the regeneration area and you know that there are going to be gaps in provision, issues of alienation or disenfranchisement, or new opportunities for creative thinking and development. Perhaps your church site is able to be used more effectively via the regeneration programme?

Whatever happens, it is really important that everyone who wants to can contribute to the visioning exercise and, indeed, throughout the whole of the process of project planning through to delivery. It is important that everyone understands what the church is working towards in the light of developments in the area. Information and communication have always been important, and they are vital if you are to enable other people to travel the journey with you. How you do this will be dependent on your church's circumstances. It may mean setting up meetings, making a DVD, having an information and contributions board at the back of the church; or it may be through open discussion fora or a housegroup network.

St John's in Peckham is a good example. They had had a new priest for a year and were looking to develop a ministry and mission strategy that was creative, sustainable, and in line with their agenda of social justice and inclusivity, but which also stretched them to consider new ideas and think 'outside the box'. Peckham has undergone some remarkable regeneration initiatives and will continue to do so for some time into the future. The church wanted to be a part of this and were seeking ways to join in that would really affect the local people, empowering them in new ways and providing a community venue that was versatile, would be accessible to a wide range of people and activities, and that would help to develop the capacity of local people, enhance local aspirations, and offer to them new experiences of the arts, both in terms of Christian productions and secular activities. The vision linked with creative and artistic regeneration initiatives being carried out in the area and worked alongside the agenda of the local authority, which was keen to develop new creative sites in the Peckham area.

St John's decided to hold a vision day for its Parochial Church Council (PCC) members to explore who they were, what they wanted to be, and how they wanted to demonstrate this. As the vision day progressed, a timeline was produced that placed their thinking into context and showed the important moments in the life of the worshipping and wider community. This helped to honour history, confirm key strengths within the parish, and siphon out weaker moments and activities.

They followed this with some 'blue-sky' thinking whereby anything and everything could be listed down as possibilities to consider. Some of these were easy to remove from the list later on, some were realistic, and some were things that might be possible in the future but not now.

A simple SWOT analysis (strengths, weaknesses, opportunities and threats) was then undertaken by the group, which honed their thinking.

Based on this information, St John's were able to produce actionable points to move the vision on. These points then influenced the formation of task groups that reported to the PCC on a regular basis and also to the church congregation, ensuring that all members were fully informed as to how things were going and how and when they had opportunities to contribute to the wider plans and work being undertaken.

As the project began to take shape and further explorations were made, the founding vision became a tool for ensuring that the group were always able to refer back, and any digressions were able to be quashed or incorporated accordingly.

The creative energies of the group, coupled with the research they had carried out, provided the basis for their project development strategy.

Building a team

This was a vital part of the work being undertaken by St John's, for this team was going to have to do some hard work to enable the sharing of the work and vision. They also needed to have some of the skills that were going to be needed to formulate the project proposal. St John's recruited volunteers from both the PCC membership and among interested people from the congregation to work with a churchwarden and with the parish priest. Once the framework of the project plan had been pulled together, the team broke into pairs to carry out specific tasks between meetings, and the results were then brought back to the next whole-group meeting for integration into the main proposal.

The team was responsible for ensuring that all of the correct information was being gathered, that all information was being recorded accurately, that networks and partnerships were functioning well, and that consultation and communication was clear and correct.

Networks and relationships

Partnership working can be an effective way of churches delivering projects in the local community, but they can be tricky too, and one needs to enter into them wisely. There are two main questions that I always advise people to explore when considering partnership working: 'How does their work and vision fit with yours?' and 'Do you have compatible values bases?'

The church will need to ensure that it is not working to someone else's agenda entirely, and that it keeps its own identity; that its resources will be used respectfully and within the guidelines of its PCC's usage agreements; that any arrangements are not going to be so short term that they jeopardize the church's ability to sustain delivery of projects; and that the partnership doesn't disrupt arrangements with other groups to which the church wants to continue to relate.

The prospective partner will need to consider whether it wants to work with an organization that belongs to one particular faith group, or work with an organization that is, perhaps, unused to delivering services to a rigorous standard, unfamiliar with evaluation processes, and unclear about funding, the meaning of regeneration language, and legislation.

However, if both organizations have the same commitment to the community, the same values base, and the same level of passion for the project, then it can work. Investing in careful preparation is time well spent for all parties. Identifying what each partner brings, allowing for difference, and thinking together about how partnership can be managed, will help everyone to jump any hurdles that get in the way.

Having clear terms of reference that state what you are about, why you are together, and how you intend to work, will formalize the partnership arrangements until such time as contracts or agreements are signed by both parties. These terms of reference often continue to be useful after formal contracts have been signed.

Partnership working can strongly benefit the communities of regeneration areas because it promotes a cohesive service that embraces local needs. Partnerships increase opportunities for churches as they strengthen resources, funds, information and skills. What churches have to offer regeneration areas is a deep local knowledge and established commitment to the community, regardless of developments, and the very real benefit of community space that is well located and known. They can also offer a strong volunteer base: a vital ingredient when delivering community-based services. Church spaces also offer a community a 'safe place', that tacit benefit of being an 'OK' place, an 'independent' place where there is an unspoken trust. These are huge contributory factors in the regeneration of communities that the church can bring beside the ethical and independent thinking that contributes so much in the discussions.

Mapping and consultation

This is something that all projects need to undertake, creating a summary of services, opinion and need in the area. You need to check out what is in your area and which people have it. What other facilities offer similar services, how are they perceived, and is there a need for more? Important questions for you to ask yourself are: 'Where can this church add value to the regeneration that is taking place?' 'Where are the gaps?' 'What do the local community want?' and 'Is it realistic?'

This can seem daunting to begin with, but once you get going it is a very exciting process:

> I would say the consultation we staged in Gipsy Hill between January and April 06 was the single most valuable piece of parish outreach I have conducted since arriving in 2001. Whether or not a brick of our hall is altered (which we hope it will) the process has been worthwhile. (The vicar of Christ Church, Gipsy Hill)

Embarking on a major refurbishment of their hall for wider community use, Christ Church Gipsy Hill sent out a questionnaire that had a relatively poor response. They then considered recruiting a consultant to carry out the work for a more fruitful response, but as there were many 'live' community links in the church community already, they decided to carry it out themselves and are so glad that they did.

Approaches were made to ten community groups including: police, junior school Parent Teacher Association, Sure Start, local councillors, and residents' groups. Each focus group consultation session was hosted by two people, refreshments were served, and all comments were recorded. A large-scale map was displayed and specific possibilities for the area were discussed and gaps highlighted, along with the implications of any developments. During this period of consultation an innovative cabaret evening with home-grown music and comedy acts also asked the audience to consider some questions about the area, and this proved to be a worthwhile and fun way of building up enthusiasm and local knowledge around the project's development.

The church is well placed in any area, but perhaps especially so in regeneration areas, to improve access to its buildings and open up a 'shared space' that the community can use. In regeneration areas there is, increasingly, a lack of social infrastructure, and more often than not there is no shared community space for local people. This whole issue is enormous in its own right, because a lack of community space means increased isolation for people, reduced choices and lack of services for local people. Regeneration can mean taking away things from local communities as well as giving to them. The church needs to be aware of this and to speak up about what this means for each particular place. Being an informed church is crucial.

Data analysis

Once you have gathered all the information from your church, your local community, and all the other necessary groups, you will need to analyse it. The experience of Gipsy Hill may help you here too: 'The main challenge of the process concerned how to use and refine the statistics we built up from the groups – the single biggest issue has been the volume of suggestions that people thought it would be good to do.'

While being open in consultation, with a flexible and organic approach, it is important to have some boundaries around the realistic possibilities if you want to present clear findings for your project bid or business plan. Both qualitative and quantitive data is valuable. You may find that as a church you are better at the qualitative side and that your partners or other agencies are able to help you with the quantitive statistics, as they often have to have gathered huge amounts of data in this area. I am a great believer in sharing information wherever possible as it saves so much time and energy for everyone. Whatever the outcome of your analysis, always present it clearly. Check out with other people that they understand what you are trying to portray before you send it off to potential partners or funders. Keep it simple.

Building up your case

The steering group or project management team have now illustrated the vision, thought about possible partnership working, mapped your area to see what is available, and consulted local residents, community groups and organizations, and you have analysed and detailed this information in a format that is clear. Next you need to consider how this would all work out in reality. What are the financial implications? Would it mean rebuilding or refurbishing church property? (Don't forget to go through any organizational structures for changing buildings around if that is relevant to you.) If it is a large project, then you may need to consider getting a feasibility study carried out. What might the budget be for equipment, staff, administrative overheads and other expenses? You will need to identify this clearly in your budget plan. (You may have had a rough ball-park figure in mind with regard to your buildings, but until you have done the appropriate research you cannot price up a project because you don't know at the outset exactly what it is going to look like.)

Now you need to plan and consider your structures of operation. Your project will need to have clear objectives, an action plan, and a way of measuring itself and what it is producing. (Any funders you have may want to contribute to this process at a later stage.) You will also need to have a financially accountable structure. Is the project part of the work done by the PCC, or are you helping to set up a not-for-profit community group or charity, or will a partner take on this role?

There will need to be a project leader, a project team, the projects network for recruiting volunteers, and the people who will be using your project. There will need to be clear roles, appropriate training, and relevant and appropriate policies set up. A visible action plan that people can contribute to may be a useful tool to ensure that your project is on target. It also helps people to work better together as a team because they can see that their contributions are valued. Consider what other forms of communication you will use to promote, include and develop your organization.You will need to ensure that all appropriate people are kept informed of your project, too, including the other voluntary, community and statutory-sector groups in your area.

You should also have some plans for an exit strategy. This may be set from the outset of your project by the funding format or by other outside influences. Wherever the deadline comes from, ensure that your team and users know about it. They can help you to plan for a successful closure to the project that is empowering for local people rather than disabling. There is nothing worse than a good project closing and the local people being unaware that this was on the cards, as this increases frustration and disillusionment.

If your project is to continue for an unspecified amount of time, you will want to keep your eye firmly on your budget, your evaluations from both users and staff, and your resources. The project may be so successful that it spawns new projects from within itself and that are grassroots grown. Fabulous if that is what happens – keep to the same principles and you should continue to flourish.

Funding

The Southwark Diocesan Funding Manager says that successful fundraising needs three things – planning, planning and planning: 'Getting your planning right at the early stages will lead to fewer problems once you start your fundraising. If you want to raise money effectively, start by investing time in planning for it properly.'

There are various ways of approaching fundraising, but breaking your fundraising needs into categories is helpful. You need a breakdown of costs. Capital costs are those items of expenditure that you don't expect to incur annually: building works, major pieces of equipment, etc. Revenue costs are the costs associated with the running of the project. There will initially be some start-up costs for launching the project and to include any legal fees you might have incurred. You will also want to consider the fixed and variable costs associated with your project and to budget for these accordingly.

You will also need to consider the type of funder that you wish to approach, and this may require some research. There are a number of main sources: the statutory sector will provide some opportunity for funding – that is, the government, the local authority, the health authority, and other bodies who handle funding on their behalf. There are trusts and foundations that provide funding; there are also corporate and private businesses that do. You might consider Lottery money, or public fundraising or, indeed, raising the finance yourself through various means.

A key point is not to rush into fundraising. You will waste valuable time starting with it at the beginning. You must have a project outline first. The creation of a business plan that incorporates all that has been said above will provide the backdrop for your fundraising plan. The Southwark Diocesan Funding Manager says:

> State what you expect to see happen when you get your project going, then list the resources you need and their costs and look at budgets and cashflows – it will be a fundraising asset. Your fundraising plan will be like a map detailing the route you are setting out on: how much you need; how you are going to raise it – and it will need to include a budget to cover the cost of fundraising, too. It should also have a timescale and be reviewed regularly to monitor how effective your fundraising is and adapt it if necessary.

My advice is: always be driven by your vision, and not by funding opportunities. Funding streams come and go and can be very much about a particular agenda. That is fine if that marries with your vision and the gaps identified through your consultation. If you go all guns blazing for a pot of money that you happen to have heard of, and it does not fit with need, resources and vision, then you are going to compromise your project or just waste your time and energy. Please do things the right way round. Don't do worthy work that is then wasted.

Like others who have walked this journey before you, you will now have a business plan that lays out exactly what you want to do. And when you have received your funding you can pick up your action plan, do your promotions and marketing, get organized with staffing, purchasing equipment, renting spaces, ensuring the admin system is set up, etc. Then comes the big day – first day of operation. There really is nothing like it. Seeing the first people walk through the door of your new project!

Clearly you will need to monitor various outputs for your funders, and you will want to receive feedback from the people who are coming along to your project. You will want to ensure that some representatives from your users are on the management or steering group, as they will be able to help you to develop the direction of the project further. All of this, along with good strategic development plans, positive working relationships with your partners, and a continued desire to provide a service to the local community, will enhance your project's sustainability.

Many churches that I have worked with in the past have felt somewhat daunted by the thought of engaging in regeneration in their neighbourhoods. I can understand why. The jargon can be incomprehensible, the stream of papers and meetings is endless, and the thought that if you dip your toe into this particular pond it might just suck you in can be quite daunting. Yet while there will be the inevitable paperwork and meetings to attend, if this is managed well, it can be an exciting time for the church and a huge opportunity for learning and sharing for all concerned. The value systems that faith groups bring to the table of regeneration discussion are most important, and some people may see this as being a critical part of their engagement, regardless of whether a project takes off in their church buildings or not. There is a role for the local church to ensure that economic forces are not the only ones around – that fairness, justice, compassion, love and hope are also demonstrated and heard on behalf of the community.

Regeneration and the role and work of the Church go together, either in working together and providing community resources and becoming partners, or in taking more of an advocacy role for the community in which the regeneration will take place.

Often the priest or other church leaders will take on some of this work, but not always – and not alone. It is important that congregations, with their skills, expertise, time, convictions and local knowledge, also find ways of supporting or challenging those who sit around the tables of decision-making. Empowered congregations who embrace and motivate their community networks and relationships to inform debate and take action are a powerful and influential group of people.

As I said at the beginning of this chapter, where regeneration brings in massive housing developments, large offices and the like, the church may be the only organization that offers opportunity and space for the human needs of a community. A touching place. Think about it!

The scope of opportunity and challenge is tremendous for the Church in regeneration areas. We will need to call on the Holy Spirit to help us, for we will need wisdom, courage and strength. We may even have to be prepared for battle on occasion, but the fruits of love, joy, hope and peace are ones that can flourish in the orchard of regeneration if we dare to engage. Imagine your church buildings being open every day and full of people benefiting from them and what goes on there. Take it from me that this is an exciting privilege. So if the opportunity to engage in regeneration comes your way, I urge you to explore it.

Further reading

Buonfino, A. and Mulgan, G. (eds), *Porcupines in Winter*, Young Foundation, London, 2006.

Church of England, *Mission-shaped Church: Church Planting and Fresh Expressions of Church in a Changing Context*, Church House Publishing, London, 2004.

Commission on Urban Life and Faith, *Faithful Cities: A Call for Celebration, Vision and Justice*, Church House Publishing/Methodist Publishing House, London, 2006.

Lawrie, A. (ed.), *The Complete Guide to Creating and Managing New Projects for Voluntary Organisations*, 2nd edn, Directory of Social Change, London, 2002.

Simmons, M. (ed.), *Street Credo: Churches in the Community*, Lemos and Crane, London, 2000.

Skinner, S. and Wilson, M., *Assessing Community Strengths*, Community Development Foundation Publications, London, 2002.

Note

1 Department for Communities and Local Government, *Firm Foundations: The Government's Framework for Community Capacity Building*, Communities and Local Government Publications, London, 2004.

14. Thinking Wider

Coping with the Thames Gateway

MALCOLM TORRY

The circumference of the city shall be eighteen thousand cubits. And the name of the city from that time on shall be, The Lord is There. (Ezekiel 48.35)

The preceding chapters have all focused on particular development projects, individual parishes or individual communities. This chapter looks a little wider: across the Thames Gateway.

If you look at a map of the Thames Gateway, it looks a bit like a pair of jaws stretching out from London towards the North Sea: the upper jaw from the Lee Valley to Southend, and the lower jaw from Deptford to Sittingbourne.

What unites the Thames Gateway is the Thames Estuary and the government's interest in lots of empty land ripe for development; but whether there is any real coherence about what's going on in the many communities strung out along the north and south banks of the estuary is a question that readers might like to consider while working through this chapter.

I don't intend to cope with the whole of the Gateway. In fact, I shall deal with only a very small part of it: from Greenwich to Thamesmead along the south bank of the Thames. This is because it's the part I know best because my experience of it stretches across 30 years, and also because in 2004 I was asked to work with the Archdeacon of Lewisham on matters relating to that part of the Thames Gateway that lies in the Diocese, and it's therefore my business to know what's going on in this small part of the Gateway.

The best way to discover what's going on here is to take the 177 bus from Deptford to Thamesmead. I recommend it. Sit on the top deck and look around you. You will find yourself thinking about many of the issues facing the Thames Gateway's communities and asking how the Church might relate to the changes taking place. You will find yourself wondering what it will all look like in 50 years' time and what it will be like to live there.

Areas

From Deptford to Greenwich

The bus approaches Deptford Bridge along New Cross Road, and ahead of you is Deptford Bridge Docklands Light Railway (DLR) station, perched high above the road. The line connects Lewisham to Greenwich and then Bank, Tower Gateway and Stratford, and thus connects a large part of south-east London to the employment opportunities offered by Canary Wharf, and soon by Stratford City as well, an office and retail development to be built around the transport interchange at Stratford. And this line will of course connect south-east London to the Olympic Games site around Stratford, and to the new international railway terminal there. It is these transport links that are transforming Lewisham and Greenwich. Before the DLR came, and North Greenwich Jubilee Line station came to the Greenwich Peninsula, there was Network Southeast – and that was all. The trains were infrequent, slow and unreliable; people who worked in the City, in the West End and in Canary Wharf preferred to live in North London; house prices were low; and people who grew up in Westcombe Park could afford to buy houses in Charlton. No longer, for most of them. Now only Abbey Wood and Thamesmead are affordable, and soon they won't be – for the same reason: Woolwich is about to get a Docklands Light Railway station and possibly Crossrail: a fast rail connection right across London from Ebbsfleet in the east to Heathrow in the west.

The bus turns left and heads towards Greenwich, passing Norman Road on the left: home of prestigious low-rise office buildings for BPTW (the architects designing Thames Gateway projects) and Grant Saw solicitors (relocating from the Royal Standard shopping area in Westcombe Park). To the right and the left along Greenwich High Road are derelict small businesses interspersed with newly built flats – and signs of transition from the one to the other: steel girder frameworks, hoardings and cranes. The tiniest patch of spare land contains a new development. To the left, above the houses, are some higher cranes where a 1960s local authority estate is being transformed into a new development. And then – you can't miss it – Novotel: brazen, modern, brick, poking out well in front of the existing building line and hiding the fine nineteenth-century architecture of Greenwich Station. Novotel is already a success: high occupancy rates, conferences, receptions and other functions. This is Greenwich's new industry: entertainment.

As you pass the station, look left, and you might see a DLR train disappearing into the tunnel which will take it to the Cutty Sark station and under the river to Canary Wharf. On the right is the cinema, now open again, in spite of the existence of the 14-screen Odeon on the Greenwich Peninsula – and there are more cinemas planned for inside The O2 (formerly the Millennium Dome). To the left is the Portman Building Society, which used to be the Greenwich Building Society: the small and local swallowed by the large and less than local; and on the right there is the Ibis Hotel, Café Rouge, and up behind it Greenwich Theatre, doing well. Then you pass the open market, with development plans hanging over it.

St Alfege's Church has its back to the street. Hawksmoor built a fabulous building, but the door is to the courtyard behind, not out on to the rest of the world. And then there are numerous cafés and restaurants, on both sides of the street. It's a combination of students and money that keeps them all going.

A glimpse of the *Cutty Sark*, and then the Old Royal Naval College is ahead of you. Now that the navy has left, these wonderful buildings have become the University of Greenwich and Trinity College of Music. Greenwich's second industry is education.

A narrow alley on the right leads to the covered market. Here the owners, the Greenwich Hospital trust, have increased the rents rapidly, putting small businesses at risk. (The trust funds a private boarding school.) They had suggested that they wanted to re-develop it, but Greenwich Borough Council have made it clear that that's not on the agenda. There is therefore less reason for forcing out the tenants, so now we hope to see a period of rent stability.

On the right there's another new conference centre, and then the National Maritime Museum and the Queen's House; and then to the left a view of the river between the Painted Hall and the Chapel of the Old Royal Naval College. We hope for similar wide views of the river between new developments, but recent experience isn't encouraging.

East Greenwich

The 1930s tenements are themselves a wave of regeneration. They were built as the slums were cleared. Behind them, Greenwich Power Station, which supplies electricity to the London Underground, dwarfs some ancient almshouses – both signs of progress in their own times. The Arches Leisure Centre on the right is soon to be demolished to make way for more new flats, and its replacement is planned for the centre of East Greenwich where new flats can be built on top of it. And then, through a gap in Trafalgar Road's rather dingy shops, you can see an old chapel, now offices; and then Christ Church – or rather, what was Christ Church, and is now the

Forum@Greenwich, a centre for integrated living and a hive of community activity. The new bit tagged on the end is where the church now meets. More shops follow, with rather a high proportion of bookies.

Last year the Woolwich Equitable Building Society closed, so that there are now no banks in East Greenwich. Derek Clacey, vicar of Christ Church, was part of the high-profile campaign that tried to stop the closure, but to no avail.

After Blackwall Lane, which leads to the Greenwich Peninsula, comes a local authority estate that is among the 10 per cent most deprived areas in the UK; on the right, Greenwich District Hospital has just been demolished to make way for a new town square for East Greenwich, with a new health centre, library, council offices, leisure centre, and flats above. The new hospital in Charlton is in serious debt because it was financed by a Private Finance Initiative.

On the left there are two funeral directors, next door to each other – and not much business for either of them now that the hospital has gone. Many of the shops here are shuttered, but not the Meridian Press, the printing shop that printed the draft copies of the chapters you're reading so that their authors could read and discuss them before finishing them off. And there are more new flats packed close together on the site of a school that has moved to the peninsula.

Ahead is a flyover. Before the 1960s, traffic reached the single Blackwall Tunnel along a narrow residential road, but increasing traffic volumes led to the second tunnel being built and a motorway-width road from Blackheath to the tunnel. (It was always intended to continue the dual carriageway to the dualled A2, and this happened 15 years ago when the Rochester Way Relief Road was built.) The Angerstein Hotel to the right of the road was almost a casualty of the new road, but a campaign to save it succeeded, which is why there's now a kink in the tunnel approach road. And the kink is the reason for St George's Hall still being there. It was compulsorily purchased from the parish church because it was where the road was to be built. When the road wasn't built there, the parish couldn't afford to buy the hall back, so it became the home of a decorating company. Interestingly symbolic, this passing of a building from religious use to aborted public use, and then to private use. Also on the right is Westcombe Park Police Station. This used to be open to the public and now isn't, and there are rumours that it's to be sold. There's now a trend towards a few large new stations for centralized functions and very small local ones for community-based Safer Neighbourhoods Teams – so this medium-sized one will go.

On the left of Woolwich Road is the half-derelict library, soon to be replaced by a new one on the old hospital site – with flats above.

At the time of writing there are roadworks on the roundabout under the flyover, and the plan is to improve pedestrian access from East Greenwich to the Greenwich Peninsula. An important concern relating to new developments is that they will be isolated from existing communities and thus foster social division and mutual suspicion. Parents and children have experienced serious difficulty walking from East Greenwich to their relocated school on the peninsula, and East Greenwich residents haven't found it easy to walk to Sainsbury's, Comet and B & Q: the retail development at the southern end of the peninsula. The new pedestrian routes, paid for by the developer, Meridian Delta Ltd, will address this problem, as will the new 129 bus route and the re-routing of an existing bus route through the shops. That's what the roadworks on the roundabout sliproad are all about.

After the roundabout, the road goes under a railway bridge. This doesn't look like an unusual bridge, but it is, because it's a private-goods line taking trains from the national rail network to an aggregates yard. No doubt the yard will one day disappear under new housing, offices, shops or light industry, but while there is construction going on in the area it will probably stay, as it's really rather useful to have a river and train terminus here and sufficient land to store mountains of roadstone, gravel and other building materials.

Before the roundabout is the old East Greenwich Fire Station, now a hotel – not of the expensive variety. After the railway bridge and a row of filthy house fronts (the result of heavy traffic rumbling past their front doors) comes the new fire station, and then ASDA, Boots, Clarks, Carphone Warehouse, Wickes, Makro and many others – except that to get to most of them from here you have to walk. The entrance to the huge car-park is round the other side. For much of this frontage there is a gap between the shops and the road. This might be used by a 'rapid transit' route from Thamesmead to North Greenwich: that is, a road that only buses can use. The road might one day become a tramline. It's all part of the plan to connect places with one another and to connect people to employment opportunities, entertainment, education and shops.

Charlton

Then on the left comes an example of a rapidly expanding industry: self-storage. Homes are getting smaller and people have more things, and the obvious answer is to build rooms to rent in a warehouse – though that isn't the only obvious answer of course. And after that there are more shops: Halfords, Currys, MFI, PC World. More places to buy the things that will get stored in the self-storage.

And on the right there's a 1980s local authority estate: that period's regeneration, except that they didn't use that word for it. Some derelict land on the left will probably soon be more flats.

After the sign to the Thames Barrier comes the Co-op funeral service's south-east London headquarters with its mortuary and garage. There might be a tragic connection between the sign and the mortuary if ever the Thames Barrier fails when we need it. The barrier is now needed more frequently than when it was built, and because the sea level is rising and the barrier is getting older, we shall soon need a replacement if we are not one day to see London flooded. Everything to the east of the barrier is of course entirely unprotected except for the inadequate walls, the newly created artificial high ground, and pumping stations. This is an important issue for people moving into the new parts of Thamesmead – and an even more important issue for those who might move into new housing along the north Kent coast. Our ancestors didn't build on these marshes, and they had good reasons for not doing so.

Woolwich

Up to the right, perched on the hill above Woolwich Dockyard railway station, is St Michael's Church: architecturally important, and with a congregation of a dozen, it is one of the best maintained church buildings in the area. A hundred years ago money was left in a will to form an independent trust fund for the maintenance of this building. The sizeable income from the substantial capital can be used for nothing else; and because the building is listed, the congregation find it hard to make changes to the building. Even a disabled toilet that cannot be seen from the nave took a long time and much negotiation. This situation is ludicrous. It really is time for a national strategy for adapting church buildings, *including* Grade I and Grade II listed buildings – and for English Heritage to support such a strategy and the Victorian Society and other such bodies to lose a lot of the influence they've got. Until the last century the regeneration of church buildings meant their adaptation. It wasn't always done well, but that's no reason for not trying to get it right now. A beautiful interior is still a beautiful interior without its fixed pews; and a beautiful exterior is still a beautiful exterior with carefully designed additions. The adaptations in the next church building, St Mary's Woolwich, could have been done better, but at least during the 1960s the attempt was made to make the space useful for local healthcare and other organizations and to provide a flexible space for worship.

To the left of the road is a rare view of the river, and then some new apartments: orange and grey. Coloured exteriors have made a comeback, especially in the Greenwich Millennium Village where the blocks of flats really do look as if they're made out of Lego. And then comes the Woolwich Ferry, and on a bad day lorries queue up around the roundabout and back along the road. The old cinema to the right is now the New Wine Church: huge membership, several pastors (Dr Tayo's ministry is international), and the home of 'Careerbuilders' – a whole-lifestyle approach to Christian discipleship, including finding you a job. This church has a growing interest in the surrounding community and in relating to other churches, and churches like this one are clearly going to be important future partners in community renewal.

At the ferry roundabout the 177 turns right to wind through Woolwich Town Centre. You will therefore miss Waterfront, a diverse leisure centre with a swimming pool very suitable for children of all ages; and you will miss the car-park and path next to the river. But you will see a town centre that has seen better times and thinks it will see them again, for Tesco is coming. Already the council offices that will be demolished to make way for Tesco are being emptied. And to Marks and Spencer will be added coffee shops, the usual chainstores, and all the paraphernalia of a vibrant shopping experience. But for the time being the centre of attention is the market stalls and the small fairground for young children.

As I write, the north side of Woolwich Arsenal railway station is a building site and the down platform is closed. This is where the new DLR station will be. The line will travel under the Thames and link up with the new connection to London City Airport. The Woolwich and Plumstead area will then experience the benefits and disbenefits of a particular kind of regeneration: people working in financial institutions in Canary Wharf and the City wanting to live here, house prices rising, and local people unable to afford to stay, particularly if they've just managed to buy a small property and they need extra space for children. They will join the exodus to Abbey Wood and then, when that goes up-market with the arrival of Crossrail, to the Medway Towns. It's the DLR that is bringing Tesco.

As the bus emerges from the town centre, back on to the lower road, there's a high wall on the other side of the road. This is the Royal Arsenal site. For centuries armaments were manufactured here. Now it's expensive flats and a few expensive houses, the Firepower Museum (the new Royal Artillery Museum, which has just been bailed out by Greenwich Borough Council), Start (flexible spaces and support services for new businesses) and the Heritage Centre: the borough's museum and local history library. It's a pity that the high wall remains. It divides the new housing from the town centre and local authority estates on the south side of the road. It creates two communities rather than one. The wall ought to have been demolished.

Then on the left is the bus garage and on the right is Plumstead railway station: both essential pieces of the transport infrastructure on which all regeneration relies. The more people travel by bus, DLR, tube and train, the more we shall slow climate change, the more we shall reduce pollution, the faster journey times will be, and the more we shall know ourselves to be a single society and a single community. Buses are now more frequent and more reliable and there are more routes than there used to be: but they're still too expensive, as is the Tube. Either the congestion charge has to be brought at least out to Woolwich (from 8 a.m. to 9.30 a.m. every day, if not for longer) or the buses have to be much cheaper and even more frequent – or both. If not, the lower road will be stationary more often than it is, and maybe one day the traffic will never move again.

Plumstead

Plumstead High Street is small shops, terraced houses, and side streets with terraced houses. Apart from the traffic levels and the new police station, it's all much as it's looked for the past 100 years. Other recent additions are the places of worship in Woolwich and Plumstead: two Sikh Gurdwaras, a Hindu Temple, and a Mosque. And then on the left is the ancient parish church, St Nicholas's Plumstead, across the village green.

Abbey Wood

The 177 turns left into Basildon Road, and then straight on into Eynsham Drive and over the railway into the Abbey Wood Estate: a 1960s regeneration project (though they didn't use that word), built on drained marshland to house people displaced by slum clearance. There's space here. Houses have gardens, albeit small ones; and you can see how many tenants have exercised their right to buy. And in the centre of the estate there's a row of shops, the parish church, and the 'Neutral Ground' project: a contact centre to enable separated fathers (mainly fathers) to relate to their children in supervised surroundings. This project was started by the parish church as its contribution to community-building. They saw a need and they set out to fulfil it.

Thamesmead

Left at the roundabout and into Thamesmead along Harrow Manor Way. At the roundabout there's a Lidl supermarket, a veterinary hospital, and a car-wash. Thamesmead was built for the car: wide dual carriageways cross it, and a motorway-style junction sits right in the middle. The nearest railway station is Abbey Wood, there's no tube or DLR, and the buses wind slowly through the residential roads. Here tower blocks are being refurbished, and new homes are being built for sale, for shared ownership, and for rent. Here you can tell the houses where tenants have exercised their right to buy by the stone cladding on them. And there's a travellers' site, with stationary mobile homes in which live some of the longest-standing residents of Thamesmead.

There's a separate chapter about Thamesmead in this book so I shall say no more about it – except that it is where the 177 terminates. To get out of Thamesmead you need to catch another bus to Abbey Wood station – and that too winds slowly through the residential roads.

The Church's response?

So what is the Church doing about it all?

The Church is responding locally. To take just a few examples: in East Greenwich, Christ Church has worked with the Greenwich Society (a local voluntary organization) to hold meetings to enable local people to discuss new developments: the hospital site, pockets of housing such as the one on the old school site, and Lovell's Wharf. The latter is a riverside site that you won't see from the top of the 177 bus, but which is important locally: the developers' first planning application was for two towers of more than 30 storeys. A meeting was held and its views were heard – along with lots of similar views – and a second application didn't have the towers in the plans. The cynical among us might say that the developers put the towers in knowing that they wouldn't get permission for them, but also that they would attract local anger, leaving less anger for the *second* application which, while without the towers, is still for a very high-density development and will cause considerable traffic congestion in East Greenwich's narrow and already crowded streets. But still, it was important to hold meetings to enable local views to be heard; and it was equally important to oppose the closure of the local branch of the Woolwich Equitable, even though it closed anyway.

In Charlton, the rector of Charlton and his ecumenical colleagues are chaplains to ASDA; in Woolwich, the Church School is being rebuilt to make room for children from the Woolwich Arsenal development and to enable people from new and old communities to meet one another; and, in general, people from new developments joining existing congregations enables communities to relate to one another.

More widely, archdeacons and Diocesan Thames Gateway officers from the different parts of the Thames Gateway meet twice a year to exchange information and good practice; and there have been occasional ecumenical gatherings.

There is no one way for the Church to relate to new and changing communities. There are many ways. Some will be pastoral; some will be prophetic; some will be both. Some ways of relating will have more predictable outcomes and some will be highly risky. It's our job as the Church, through prayer and consultation, to work out what seems to be the right approach for the new and changing communities we're in – and then to take the risk of acting on that decision.

Issues facing the Thames Gateway

There has always been regeneration in the Thames Gateway. The current phase is simply this century's new developments, responding to the needs of society and the economy, and largely driven by construction companies wanting to make some money and local authorities wanting to see populations rise and council tax receipts go up: perfectly reasonable desires.

But if it isn't all to end in tears then a few issues need to be addressed:

Is it really sensible to build in the flood plain? Might the lack of drinking water in the South-east become a reason for shifting economic activity, and therefore homes, elsewhere in the UK? Are the building densities we are now seeing in the London part of the Thames Gateway good for people? How can we ensure that existing and new communities belong to one another? How can new and renewed built environments encourage real social mixing? Is it responsible to build new homes when there really isn't sufficient *public* transport infrastructure? When is government going to brave the anger of motorists and benefit society as a whole by *forcing* people to reduce car use? Section 106 of the Town and Country Planning Act 1990 enables the planning authority to enter into an agreement with a developer over any issue related to the planned development. So, for instance, a supermarket developer can be asked to pay for a new road layout made necessary by the development; or an arena developer can be asked to pay for a controlled parking zone in nearby streets; or the developer of a new residential area can be asked to pay for buildings for healthcare or for pedestrian access or public transport alterations. There is some good practice available on the use of such Section 106 agreements to ensure adequate provision of community spaces for education, socializing, community development, youth provision, elderly people's provision, and worship spaces for faith communities. How is such good practice to become more universal? Is the piecemeal approach to new developments – including those in the Thames Gateway – going to be sustainable if there is no overall strategy for providing sufficient educational facilities, healthcare facilities and, above all, transport infrastructure? In East Greenwich there's a dozen new developments, the Greenwich Peninsula is being built all over, and the Olympic Village, Stratford City and much more is to be built north of the river. These are all planned separately and their traffic impacts are separately evaluated. There seems to be little understanding that *together* they will have a significant impact on traffic volumes, pollution levels and climate change.

So what are the issues facing the Church?

In new and changing communities the Church has a responsibility to worship God and to serve those communities – and I put the tasks in that order advisedly. If the Church is not a worshipping community, then it is not the Church, so spaces in which to worship are essential. These need not belong to any particular church, and increasingly they will be shared with other faith communities and with secular uses – but they must be available for worship, and prayer and worship must be accessible and inclusive. On the basis of its worshipping and praying, the Church will serve its community, and it will do it with other groups, both religious and secular. An important part of serving a new community is serving the people building it, which means organizing a chaplaincy service to its construction companies – and then to the institutions that emerge. And if the initial stages are done together with other faith communities, then it will also be possible to serve the mature community together. This is not an invitation to the Church to lose its distinctiveness. It is a multi-faith approach that is required, not an inter-faith one, and the Church will serve a multi-faith approach most effectively if it is clear about the distinctive nature of the Christian faith and of the Church's worship and doctrine.

All of this will, of course, require resources. It will require public authorities to put in large amounts of money to ensure adequate public transport infrastructure and public services; and it will require cash-strapped churches to concentrate financial and human resources in new and changing communities. This will not be easy. It is always easiest to keep or put resources where religious institutions already exist and where existing work has a good claim on central funds and personpower. But taking the longer-term view requires the injection of additional resources in new and changing communities with a view to the emerging Christian congregations then generating their own human and financial resources, which they will if given sufficient help at the beginning – and not if they aren't.

Conclusion

To name a large area 'the Thames Gateway' is to make it sound as if there is a single project in view. There isn't. Many of the same issues might be shared across the different regeneration projects in this large area, and I have mentioned some of them above; but each part of the Gateway contains different developments, they relate to different existing communities, and they quite properly have different characters. They must all be handled individually. It is therefore appropriate to have a variety of 'delivery bodies' – government agencies (agencies of both local, regional and central government) – managing the planning process, and it is appropriate for the Church to manage its activity in each new and each changing community separately. What's important is that it can do that – and so to have each particular development in a single parish can be very helpful. Where developments cross parish boundaries it can be helpful for individuals and projects to work across those boundaries, and for clear agreements between parishes to be in place to enable this to happen. Meetings for sharing good practice are essential, and these must be denominational, ecumenical and multi-faith, for there are aspects of what we are doing that will be done separately and other aspects that will be done together.

Above all, both traditional and experimental approaches will be required. Diversity of types of development requires a variety of approaches to the Church's work, and each parish or group of parishes must be trusted to learn from others and to chart its own strategy along with its secular and religious partners. The task of diocesan authorities is to support this process, to evaluate strategies and outcomes, to encourage open communication and lots of collaboration, to ensure that people in different situations meet one another, to provide the necessary resources (where they can) and, where necessary, to pick up the pieces if things go wrong. Experiments will sometimes go wrong – but without experiment the Church will not adequately serve new and changing communities, and without experiment there might not be the new worshipping communities that new and changing communities require.

Further reading/websites

Department of Communities and Local Government: http://www. communities.gov.uk.

Section 106 agreements: http://www.idea-knowledge.gov.uk/idk/ core/page.do?pageId=71631.

Thames Gateway London Partnership: http://www.thames-gateway. org.uk.

Thames Gateway Forum: http://www.thamesgatewayforum.com.

Conclusion:
Building God's City

MALCOLM TORRY

Jerusalem, Jerusalem, the city that kills the prophets and stones those who are sent to it! How often have I desired to gather your children together as a hen gathers her brood under her wings, and you were not willing! See, your house is left to you, desolate. For I tell you, you will not see me again until you say, 'Blessed is the one who comes in the name of the Lord.' (Matthew 23.37–39)

We have a small map on our wall at home. The first suburban railways were built in South London: one stops at Greenwich because they weren't allowed to go through the park; and one loops through Blackheath on its way to Charlton, Woolwich and Dartford. Camberwell is still a village, with fields round it.

South London isn't very old, but it's already seen wave after wave of regeneration. At the Elephant and Castle slums were demolished to build flats, the flats were demolished so that the Heygate Estate could be built, and that's now to be knocked down to enable the whole area to be rebuilt.

Often there has been little planning, redevelopment has been soulless and haphazard, and problems have intensified.

When we married in 1976 we moved into a flat in Camberwell Road and watched the last blocks of the Gloucester Grove Estate being built. Those buildings got a design award. It was all just too optimistic about human nature. It hadn't occurred to the planners that teenagers might build bonfires at the bottom of the spiral staircase so that they could watch the smoke climb the stairs and blacken the internal corridors.

That area is now very different, having experienced its most recent regeneration. The planning process for any regeneration project today includes a consultation with the Metropolitan Police. Experts in crime can help the planners to 'design out' crime. 'Defensible space' is always part of the answer, the idea being that if every patch of ground is someone's responsibility and is overlooked by them and by others, then crime is less likely. There is now less optimism around, and rather more realism. Or you could say that there is more recognition of the reality of sin of both the personal and the structural varieties.

South London is no stranger to sin. For hundreds of years London has shipped across the Thames what it regarded as the less desirable side of its life: theatres, circuses, fairs, prostitutes, prisons. Until 150 years ago it was all close to the river: it was on the South Bank.

The area known as South London isn't very old and the Diocese of Southwark is only 100 years old, and the Church in South London has always been characterized by the experiment and innovation characteristic of youth. Only a Church willing to risk itself is going to be of any use in a fast-changing environment, and there has never been a period when South London hasn't experienced significant change. The evidence contained in the chapters of this book reveals a Church still willing to take the necessary risks.

These risks must now surely be taken in two directions:

First, the Church must have the courage to join in: participating with the local community as it seeks answers to an area's problems; joining in planning consultations; joining tenants' action groups; joining multi-faith projects; joining partnerships of voluntary-sector groups – and putting up with the tedium of long meetings full of professional-sounding language that really isn't very professional.

Second, the Church must have the courage to ask hard questions and sometimes to say 'no': to say 'no' to projects that make it harder for poorer families to find homes near to their relatives and friends; 'no' to the loss of local shops; 'no' to a casino; 'no' to 'affordable housing' that isn't affordable; 'no' to fragmentation of communities; 'no' to gated communities;[1] 'no' to greater inequality.[2] For regeneration can mean that life gets worse, not better, for some poorer and more vulnerable people.

The Church must sometimes be a servant, sometimes a leader, sometimes an advocate, sometimes a judge, sometimes a reconciler, and sometimes a prophet asking whether we're creating a built environment that future generations will loath in the same way as 1960s tower blocks came to be loathed.[3]

Sometimes our vision of the city to come will cause us to express support for a regeneration project because we believe that the new built environment and the community that will emerge there will have some of the characteristics of the City of God and will therefore be a signpost promising that City. Sometimes our vision of the City to come will cause us to criticize the soulless new buildings, the divisions or the lack of diversity in the new or changing community, or the lack of involvement for local people as the changes occur.

But whichever attitude we take we must be there: in one-to-one conversations, attending evening meetings, visiting exhibitions of proposals, making appointments with planning officers and developers. We have a voice, and we must use it, as many of those portrayed in this book have done. Sometimes our voice will be heard in public meetings, and sometimes in the corridor afterwards, but speak we must – particularly on the question as to who benefits from regeneration projects and who doesn't.

When I say that it's the *Church* that must be involved, I mean that it must be the *Church*, the 'body'. It's all too easy for the clergy, and particularly the full-time clergy, to become 'the Church' in this context. Yes, the clergy sometimes have expertise, contacts and time, and it would be a dereliction of duty for them not to be involved, but it must never be only that. A vital piece of consultation is that which occurs among a congregation as it asks itself what it thinks and why, and what it's going to do about it.

This process can of course be quite a struggle if much of the congregation has been decanted from local authority housing prior to its demolition. If they're not far away, then they'll come back to help, and that will be welcome – but it isn't easy for a bussed-in congregation to relate to a new or changing community, and it might be right for some of the moved-away members to go in order to leave some social space in the congregation for new members to join, thus renewing both the congregation and the community.

While it remains the local responsibility to cope with new and changing communities, there are things that the wider Church can do to help. At diocesan level, moral support, the provision of the necessary staff and housing, and the reviewing of parish boundaries can all be important. And there is a case too for national resourcing of the Church in places facing massive change, and particularly when such change is happening in London.

South London currently contains three of the largest regeneration schemes in Europe either planned or being built (though the Olympics site and Stratford will soon be just as large); and London has regional, national and international significance. In this situation there is a case for a transfer of resources from the Church nationally. Yes, the parish must always take its responsibility seriously (and one thing that the Church nationally can always do is try to ensure that any large regeneration project is in a single parish, for that way responsibility is clear and effort need not be expended on parish-to-parish negotiation). But in order for spiritual capital to be built up and to become effective, human and financial resources will always be needed: for administrative staff, buildings, project start-up costs, chaplaincy staff, and contingency funds – for experiment will sometimes fail.

The aim is the well-being of the new or renewed community, a well-being that points us towards the City of God. The motivation for our involvement is our faith in the God who will bring about that City, and we must not be afraid to use the theological language of sin, hope, death and resurrection.

Above all, let us keep the Eucharist at the heart of our strategy, for, whatever else they are, the taking of bread and wine, the giving of thanks, the breaking of the bread and the sharing of bread and wine form a strategy for building an integrated and diverse community in which all are welcome and respected and in which all experience the promise of the City of God. And, whatever else it is, the Eucharist is a protest against anything that doesn't promise such a City.

Then I saw a new heaven and a new earth; for the first heaven and the first earth had passed away, and the sea was no more. And I saw the holy city, the new Jerusalem, coming down out of heaven from God, prepared as a bride adorned for her husband. And I heard a loud voice from the throne saying,

'See, the home of God is among mortals.
He will dwell with them;
they will be his peoples,
and God himself will be with them;
he will wipe every tear from their eyes.
Death will be no more;
mourning and crying and pain will be no more,
for the first things have passed away.'

And the one who was seated on the throne said, 'See, I am making all things new.' (Revelation 21.1–5)

This is our hope. Will the city that we are building inspire that hope, or will it be the kind of city that Jesus wept over? Will regeneration bring renewal?

I pray that our city will be a city that promises us the City of God.

Further reading

Butler, T. with Robson, G., *London Calling: The Middle Classes and the Remaking of Inner London*, Berg, Oxford, 2003.

Furbey, R. and Macey, M., 'Religion and Urban Regeneration: A Place for Faith?' *Policy and Politics*, vol. 33, no. 1, 2000, pp. 95–116.

Hamnett, C., *Unequal City: London in the Global Arena*, Routledge, London and New York, 2003.

Notes

1 See Glancey, J., 'The Re-generation Game: What's Really Happening to Our Cities?', *Re-generation*, Royal Society of Arts, 27 October 2004, on the commodification of dwellings. Dwellings are become investments rather than homes, and this is something to which the Church might wish to say 'no'.

2 On increasing inequality, see Hamnett, C., *Unequal City: London in the Global Arena*, Routledge, London and New York, 2003. On the increasingly middle-class nature of inner London, see Butler, T. with Robson, G., *London Calling: The Middle Classes and the Remaking of Inner London*, Oxford, Berg, 2003.

3 See Furbey, R. and Macey, M., 'Religion and Urban Regeneration: A Place for Faith?', *Policy and Politics*, vol. 33, no. 1, 2000, pp. 95–116, on some of the different roles that faith communities can play in relation to regeneration projects.

Glossary

Accredited ministry
A ministry recognized by the bishop of a diocese by the granting of a licence or commission.

Alpha course
A course of study for enquirers published by Holy Trinity, Brompton. The course consists of a series of evenings during which participants share a meal, listen to a talk, and hold a discussion. There might also be a weekend about the Holy Spirit.

Altar
A table at which, according to Jesus' command, bread and wine are taken, thanks is given, bread is broken, and the bread and wine are shared. It is called an 'altar' because the stone construction on which animals were slaughtered during and before the time of Jesus was called an 'altar'.

Anglican Communion
The Anglican Communion is all those dioceses that are in communion with the Archbishop of Canterbury: in practice, all those whose bishops attend the Lambeth Conference once every ten years.

Anglicanism
A set of practices and ideas that characterize the Anglican Communion or, more specifically, the Church of England.

Annual Parochial Church Meeting (APCM)
A meeting held each year (before the end of April) at which members of the Electoral Roll vote for the Parochial Church Council (PCC), receive the accounts, and undertake other business similar to that of Annual General Meetings in other organizations. Churchwardens are also elected at the meeting.

Archdeacon
A bishop's assistant, with legal and other functions of their own but which can be delegated. An archdeacon must be in deacon's orders, but is usually a priest. In practice, an archdeacon can be a pastoral figure in the diocese.

Archdeaconry	An area in which an archdeacon is the archdeacon.
Area Dean	A new name for a rural dean.
Audit Commission	A government body charged with examining public bodies' accounts and activities to determine whether or not value for money is being obtained.
Baptism	The initiation rite for a Christian. It can be carried out at any age, but when children are baptized, godparents speak for them.
Baptist	A denomination that believes that only adults can be baptized. Also used to designate a member of that denomination.
Benefice	A parish or parishes of which a priest is incumbent.
Bishop	Someone ordained by other bishops to the first order of the Church's threefold ministry of bishop, priest and deacon. The bishop acts as a focus of unity for the diocese and cares for its people and clergy.
Canon	'Canon' has two meanings: a) the title of a cathedral dignitary, either residentiary (i.e. receiving a stipend to work on the cathedral staff) or honorary (i.e. receiving a stipend for some other post, but having the right to sit in a cathedral stall); b) a rule governing the Church. The canons are revised by General Synod and agreed by Parliament.
Capital	Something built up and that can be drawn upon. See 'Social Capital' below.
Catholic	When used with 'Roman', see 'Roman Catholic' below. When used with 'Anglican', as in 'Anglo-Catholic', it means a member of the Church of England who prefers a more elaborate liturgy and holds beliefs that Roman Catholics hold. When used with 'liberal', as in 'liberal catholic', it means someone who prefers a simpler liturgy and believes some of what Anglo-Catholics believe. In the historic creeds the word means 'universal'.
Chalice	A large cup, usually of silver or silver plated, into which wine is poured at the Eucharist and from which the congregation drinks.

Chamber of Commerce	A gathering of businessmen and businesswomen from a particular borough or area to enable them to do business with one another.
Chaplain	Someone fulfilling a pastoral role in an institution, usually a hospital, factory, university, etc. The chaplain might or might not be a member of the clergy.
Chapter	A regular meeting of the clergy of a deanery that they are expected, but not obliged, to attend.
Church	With a lower case initial letter, it means a congregation of Christians or the building within which they meet. With a capital initial letter, it means the entire universal body of Christian believers and all of its local manifestations. The word can also have a capital letter if it is part of a denomination's title, as in 'Methodist Church'. In some contexts in this book, the word will start with a capital letter because it is short for 'Church of England'. The word also has a sociological meaning: see below on 'Denomination'.
Church Army	A voluntary hierarchical organization which evangelizes, runs homelessness projects, and generally lives out the gospel. Best understood as the Anglican version of the Salvation Army. Hence 'Church Army evangelist': 'evangelist' because they are commissioned as evangelists; and 'Church Army officer', which means 'Church Army evangelist'.
Church of England	A federation of dioceses in England that have bishops in communion with the Archbishop of Canterbury and, since dioceses are federations of parishes with umbrella organizations to serve them, the Church of England is a federation of parishes and of umbrella organizations.
Churches Together	Many areas have 'Churches Together' groups to which congregations of different denominations send representatives. These groups might or might not be formally constituted. There is usually a regular meeting of representatives of churches in the area, and joint projects might be planned.

Church Urban Fund	Following the publication of the *Faith in the City* report in 1985, the Church Urban Fund was set up to fund community development projects in urban priority areas.
Churchwarden	An ancient elected office. Each parish has two churchwardens elected annually. The churchwardens have a number of powers, such as the ability to veto the appointment of an incumbent, and a number of responsibilities, such as the annual completion of articles of enquiry sent by the archdeacon. They are responsible, with the incumbent, for the maintenance of public worship and the care of the church building.
Clergy	A collective noun for bishops, priests and deacons. Whether the clergy remain lay people is an interesting question. A priest remains a deacon, and a bishop remains a priest and a deacon, so it might be thought that they all remain lay people. But the Church's synodical structure separates people into bishops, other clergy, and laity.
Closed Circuit Television (CCTV)	A system of television cameras and monitors that enable the police and private security organizations to watch what is going on.
Common Worship	The name of the collection of alternative services authorized for use in the Church of England in 2000.
Communion	Sharing in bread and wine at the Eucharist, from which derives the meaning of 'taking communion to . . .': usually to someone who can't get out and to whom a priest or someone else takes bread and wine from the service in church. See also: 'Anglican Communion'.
Community Health Council	An independent body within the NHS, set up to look after the interests of patients, carers, and concerned individuals.
Compulsory Purchase Order	An order made by a local authority or other government body that enables it to purchase a property at the market rate whether or not the owner wishes to sell it.
Congregation	Any gathering of Christians for the purpose of worship.

Consultation   Communication with people about any proposals being made.

Conventional district   An area within one or more parishes under the care of a minister. When such a district is established, the parishes within which it lies lose most of their functions in relation to the district. Conventional districts are established where new housing and other developments occur and it isn't initially clear how parish boundaries should be reorganized.

Curacy   An assistant priest's post. An assistant priest in a parish can be either stipendiary or non-stipendiary. The term often applies to an ordained minister's first and training post where the curate is under the supervision of a training incumbent. For the first year the curate is a deacon and thereafter a priest.

Curate   Someone undertaking a curacy.

Deacon   Someone ordained by the bishop to the third order of the Church's threefold ministry of bishop, priest and deacon. The deacon's role is outlined in the Ordinal and is one of service and teaching. The deacon cannot preside at the Eucharist or be incumbent of a parish.

Deanery   An area, sometimes coterminous with a natural community or communities but not always, usually comprising a dozen or so parishes. Every deanery has a Deanery Synod (chaired by the lay chair and the area dean) and a clergy chapter (chaired by the area dean).

Deanery Synod   The governing body of a deanery.

Denomination   A federation of congregations, usually with an umbrella organization or organizations to fulfil functions best carried out centrally, such as the payment of clergy. The word also has a separate but connected meaning in the social sciences, where it means a category of religious organization between the categories of 'sect' and 'church'. The denomination has more open boundaries than a sect, but boundaries less open than for a church (with 'church' here defined in terms of characteristics such as open boundaries and diverse belief-systems, i.e. not as defined above).

Diocesan Advisory Committee   A committee of the diocese, containing elected members and members appointed for their expertise, which advises the Chancellor of the Diocese (a legal officer) whether or not to grant faculties for proposed changes to church buildings.

Diocesan missioner   Either a canon of the cathedral or someone else whose job it is to remind the parishes that mission is their responsibility. They might do some mission themselves.

Diocesan Synod   The governing body of a diocese. There are three houses: bishops, clergy, and laity. A vote by houses can be requested. The synod sets diocesan policy and the budget of the diocese. All bishops in the diocese are members, and there are elections for the house of clergy (among all clergy) and for the house of laity (the electors being Deanery Synod members).

Diocese   A federation of parishes with an umbrella organization to carry out those functions best dealt with centrally, such as the payment of clergy. The chief pastor of a diocese is its bishop (who might be assisted by suffragan or area bishops).

Diocese of Southwark   The parishes of South London and of parts of Kent and Surrey.

District   In a parish with more than one church building, districts can be established. The Parochial Church Council (PCC) can delegate to District Church Councils certain decisions relating to particular buildings, the congregations that meet in them, and the Church's mission in the communities in which the buildings are situated.

District Church Council   The governing body of a district. The Parochial Church Council (PCC) of the parish in which the district lies decides which decisions to delegate to the District Church Council.

Ecumenical borough deans   In London boroughs, and elsewhere, each denomination appoints a borough dean to represent the denomination to the local authority and other parts of civil society. The borough deans meet, and often act together.

Ecumenism   The relating of different denominations to each other at local, regional or national level.

English Heritage   A government body that makes grants for the upkeep of significant buildings and advises on the care of such buildings.

Episcopal area   Part of a diocese in which some of the diocesan bishop's functions have been delegated to an area bishop.

Eucharist   A fourfold action of taking bread and wine, giving thanks over them, breaking the bread, and sharing the bread and wine. The word's meaning generally extends to the whole event, including hymns, readings, prayers, the peace, etc.

Evangelical   A Christian or a congregation might be called evangelical if they think of the Bible as the Christian's primary authority. Evangelical worship is often informal.

Evangelist   Someone who tells the good news of the kingdom of God's coming.

Evening Prayer   An evening service containing Bible readings, canticles (biblical passages said by the congregation), and prayers.

Evensong   Evening Prayer with some parts sung, and maybe hymns added.

Exit strategy   A plan for closing down the project.

Faculty   A document giving a parish permission to alter the parish church or to undertake a particular activity within it.

Faith community   Any body of people who are adherents of a religion.

Faithful capital   See 'Spiritual capital'.

Faith hate crime   A hate crime committed where the faith tradition of the victim is a factor.

Feasibility study   A look at how practical and realistic the plans are that you are making and their impact.

Floor target The minimum standard expected by government to be attained by local authorities and their partners.

Free Church This term normally designates any denomination apart from the Church of England and the Roman Catholic Church, e.g. the Methodist Church. There are many non-affiliated congregations that can be regarded as Free Churches in their own right.

Freehold A priest who is inducted as rector or vicar (or team rector) holds the freehold of the benefice. This is a useful legal fiction. It means that the incumbent owns the parish church and the parsonage house, but can't do anything with them except look after them. (A priest who holds the freehold can stay in post until they are 70 years old.)

Functional Body The Mayor of London's Functional Bodies are: Transport for London, London Development Agency, London Fire and Emergency Planning Authority, Metropolitan Police Authority.

Gentrification The change that takes place in a neighbourhood when middle-class and affluent professionals move into working-class and inner-city areas.

Gospel The good news of Jesus and of the kingdom of God for which he hoped and which he proclaimed. 'Gospel' is also a book containing the good news of Jesus and of the kingdom of God. (In this book, a lower case g connotes the gospel message, and an upper case G one of the four Gospels.)

Healing ministry Praying for people who are ill or otherwise suffering, the prayer often being accompanied by the laying on of hands and/or anointing with oil.

Holy Communion See 'Eucharist'.

Holy Spirit The third person of the Trinity. For this and other theological terms, readers should consult a good theological dictionary.

Housing association An institution that builds housing (often funded by the government's Housing Corporation) and either rents it to tenants or offers it on a shared equity basis.

Housing Corporation	A government body that funds housing associations.
Incumbent	The priest who holds the freehold of the benefice.
Industrial chaplain	A chaplain in an industrial institution, though in practice many industrial chaplains undertake a variety of activities in connection with the Christian faith's relationship to the economy.
Industrial mission	The activity of relating the Christian faith to the world of work and to the economy. An industrial mission is an institution set up for this purpose.
Infrastructure	A system of physical structures (e.g. railway lines, roads, tunnels, etc.) that make activities possible, e.g. the 'transport infrastructure' makes transport possible.
Intercessions	Prayers, normally offered during public worship, requesting God to do things.
Inter-faith	A description of worship or other activity in which institutions and/or members of different faiths are involved. Because inter-faith activity such as joint worship might distress members of individual faith communities, such activity tends to be small-scale and for individuals committed to inter-faith work.
Keyworker housing	Housing built specifically for workers necessary to the functioning of a community (such as police officers, teachers and nurses) and often available at reduced rent or on a shared-equity basis on favourable terms.
Kingdom of God	A community of justice and peace, ruled by a just and merciful God, that Jesus came to inaugurate and for which Christians hope.
Laity	Anyone other than bishops, priests and deacons. Whether bishops, priests and deacons remain laity after their ordination is an interesting question.
Lay person	A member of the laity.
Lent call	An appeal for funds for a handful of charitable projects in the Diocese of Southwark during Lent, the penitential period before Easter.

Licence	A document giving a deacon, priest or reader permission to fulfil their ministry in a particular parish or parishes.
Liturgy	What is said and done at church services.
Local Area Agreement	An agreement struck between government, the local authority and its partners in an area (working through the Local Strategic Partnerships (LSP)) to improve public services.
Local Ecumenical Partnership	A formally constituted relationship between churches (buildings and/or congregations) of different denominations. Provision is often made for joint worship within certain limits.
Local Strategic Partnership (LSP)	Statutory, voluntary, community, faith and business sectors working together at local authority level to improve life for the most marginalized and poorest residents by improving public services. LSPs are central to the government's Neighbourhood Renewal Strategy for the 88 poorest local authorities.
Lower Layer Super Output Area (LSOA)	Small areas of around 1,500 residents used by government statisticians. Several LSOAs nest within an electoral ward.
Mapping	The writing of lists of all the services in the area
Mass	See 'Eucharist'.
Master plan (or Masterplan)	A plan covering an entire development site showing in broad outline what the new or changed built environment will look like. It will normally show the sizes and shapes of buildings, open spaces, roads and paths, etc.
Methodist Church	A denomination started by some of John Wesley's followers.
Minister	A rather loose term to refer to anyone undertaking a liturgical or pastoral function. The minister can be a bishop, a priest, a deacon, a reader, a Southwark pastoral auxiliary, or a lay person.
Mission	Going out to serve and evangelize. Hence 'mission team': a group of people in a parish or diocese trained and commissioned to do mission.

Morning Prayer	A morning service containing Bible readings, canticles (biblical passages said by the congregation), and prayers.
Multi-faith	A description of activity in which institutions and/or members of different faiths are involved. Unlike 'inter-faith', joint activities that might distress members of the faith communities involved are avoided.
Muslim	An adherent of Islam, the religion founded on the Qur'an and of which Muhammad is the final prophet.
Negative equity	If a dwelling is bought on a mortgage for price A, and B has been paid off the capital, then when it is sold the occupant has to repay to the mortgagor A minus B. If the dwelling is sold for C, then the occupant receives C minus A plus B. If this figure is negative, then the occupant is said to be in 'negative equity'.
Network	Lines of communication that link people together.
New Deal for Communities (NDC)	Part of the government's strategy to tackle multiple deprivation in the most deprived neighbourhoods in the UK, tackling their problems in an intensive and co-ordinated way.
Non-Stipendiary Minister (NSM)	A deacon or priest who does not receive a stipend. Most non-stipendiary clergy are curates and are usually designated 'honorary curate'.
Ordain, to	To make someone a deacon, priest or bishop. See 'Ordination' below.
Ordained Local Minister (OLM)	A minister ordained deacon and then priest following a diocesan training course. The licence usually restricts the minister's role to a particular parish or parishes.
Ordination	The act of making someone a deacon, priest or bishop. This is done by the bishop (or, in the case of the ordination of a bishop, bishops) laying hands on the candidate and praying that God's Spirit will give him/her the necessary grace for the office and work of the ministry in question.

Outcome   The hoped-for positive results of the activities and events that make up a regeneration project.

Output   An activity or event that is measured and monitored as part of a regeneration project.

Parish   The parish is a patch of land with its community and institutions, with a congregation or congregations, with a priest or priests, and with a building or buildings for worship.

Parish Communion   See 'Eucharist'.

Parish musician   Someone appointed by the parish to co-ordinate the music.

Parochial Church Council (PCC)   The governing body of a parish. The churchwardens and the incumbent are *ex officio* members. Members are elected from the electoral roll at the Annual Parochial Church Meeting. The Council takes all decisions relating to the life of the parish except for a few reserved to the incumbent (mainly in relation to the conduct of worship).

Pastoral   Anything to do with the care of the parish's people, or with the parish's organization or boundaries, or with the structures within which clergy operate. Hence 'pastoral auxiliary': someone appointed to do pastoral work.

Pentecost   A Jewish festival. At the Pentecost immediately following Jesus' resurrection, the Holy Spirit descended on the apostles and the Christian Church was born.

Pentecostal   A description of congregations or federations in which the spiritual gifts mentioned by Paul in 1 Corinthians 12 and 14 (and particularly speaking in tongues) are central to prayer and worship.

Permission to officiate (PTO)   A bishop's authorization of a priest to preside and preach in his diocese. Retired clergy are usually granted permission to officiate, and some others are too.

Practice-based commissioning   Originally intended to be treatments provided more locally, away from hospitals, and commissioned by local GPs according to need. Commonly, in fact, it is referral management/reduction in order to save money.

Priest Someone ordained by the bishop to the second order of the Church's threefold ministry of bishop, priest and deacon. The priest's functions are outlined in the Ordinal.

Priest in charge A priest appointed to a parish either with a fixed-term licence or with no security at all – so less in charge than a priest with the freehold.

Primary Care Trust A government appointed and funded Trust with responsibility for primary medical care.

Project proposal An outline document that states what the project will do and how it will do it.

Quinquennial survey Once every five years, every parish church has to be surveyed by an architect and a report on the building's condition presented to the incumbent and the Parochial Church Council (PCC).

Reader Someone trained in preaching and in leading worship (but not the Eucharist) and licensed by the bishop to fulfil these functions in a parish or parishes.

Rector One of the two designations of an incumbent of a parish. The other is 'vicar'. Historically, the vicar stood in for a rector.

Regeneration The process of bringing new and more vigorous life to an area or institution (see the beginning of Chapter 1).

Requiem Mass A Mass to remember and pray for the dead.

Right to buy Legislation passed in 1980 that allows tenants of local authority housing to buy the property they are renting.

Roman Catholic Church A federation of parishes and dioceses in communion with the Bishop of Rome.

Rural dean A priest appointed by the bishop to convene the clergy chapter and chair the Deanery Synod. There is some debate as to whether the rural dean is

the bishop's representative to the deanery or the
deanery's representative to the bishop. In practice,
he or she is usually a bit of both.

Sacrament   An outward and visible sign of an inward spiritual
reality. The Church of England recognizes two
sacraments: baptism and the Eucharist. Other
Churches recognize rather more.

Safer   Small, dedicated teams of police officers and Com-
Neighbour-   munity Support Officers allocated to a specific
hood Teams   ward in order to understand the local situation and
work to the priorities of local residents.

School league/ A table showing the academic performance of
performance   students in school at key stages.
table

Shared equity   Housing partly owned by its occupant and partly
housing   owned by a registered social landlord or other
body. A mortgage is normally being paid on the
part owned by the occupant, and rent is paid for
the proportion owned by the registered social
landlord or other body.

Simultaneous   A Eucharist conducted together by different
Eucharist   denominations, usually the Roman Catholic Church
and the Church of England. The Roman Catholic
rite is used, the two priests use separate altars,
and people normally receive communion from
the priest of their own denomination. Simultaneous Eucharists are rare and are in danger of
extinction.

Single   Beginning in 1994, SRBs brought together a num-
Regeneration   ber of programmes from several government
Budget (SRB)   departments with the aim of simplifying and
streamlining the assistance available for regeneration.

Social audit   Local community research, identifying the needs
and assets of a neighbourhood (for example, a
parish).

Social capital A network of relationships and capabilities built
up within a community or between communities
which can be drawn upon to satisfy the community's needs.

Social housing Housing owned by a local authority or a registered social landlord (such as a housing association) and available for rent.

Social landlord A category, including local authorities and housing associations, that rents housing to tenants (normally on the basis of an assessment of need for housing).

Spiritual capital A network of spiritual relationships (within, outside and between congregations) and of spiritual capabilities (of individuals and communities) on which individuals and communities can draw to satisfy spiritual needs.

Stipend What parochial clergy are paid. It is not a salary as there is no contract of employment. The payment is intended to enable the priest and his/her family to live without anxiety and thus to be of service to the parish.

Stock transfer The transfer of housing stock from local authorities to registered social landlords.

Stretch Target A public service target that, if met by a local authority and its partners, is rewarded by government with extra funding.

SureStart A government programme to deliver the best start in life for every child. It brings together early education, childcare, health and family support.

SWOT analysis A list of strengths, weaknesses, opportunities and threats that are pertinent to the subject.

Synod A gathering of elected and *ex officio* members for deliberation and decision-making. The Church of England has synods at the parish level (Parochial Church Council (PCC)), the deanery level (Deanery Synod), the diocesan level (Diocesan Synod), and the national level (General Synod).

Synodical Anything to do with synods.

Tate Modern A modern art gallery built inside the old Bankside Power Station on the south bank of the Thames.

Team ministry A team of clergy, comprising a team rector and team vicar(s), serving a parish or parishes. The team rector is the incumbent, and the team vicar(s) are not. They are all told that they are of incumbent status.

Team rector Every team ministry has a team rector who is expected to fulfil a co-ordinating role. The team rector holds the freehold of the benefice for a limited period, usually for seven years. The team rector is not a rector.

Team vicar Every team ministry has one or more team vicars. A team vicar is of 'incumbent status', as is the team rector. The team vicar is not a vicar, but can be designated vicar of a particular parish or district.

Terms of reference This is a document that says what your group is about and how individuals/groupings agree to operate together.

Thames Gateway A great deal of empty land ripe for development on both sides of the Thames estuary, along with existing communities adjacent to it. In South London, the Thames Gateway includes Thamesmead, Woolwich, the north end of Charlton and the Greenwich Peninsula.

Theology Words about God.

Title That part of a curacy that has to be completed before a priest can be appointed to a post with responsibility. It is usually two years for a stipendiary curate and four years for a non-stipendiary curate or Ordained Local Minister (OLM).

Town centre management The division of London boroughs into smaller 'towns' which manage some of their own public services and encourage investment.

Unitary development plan A statutory document that sets out a local authority's planning policies and that will be used to guide development, conservation, regeneration and environmental improvement activity.

United Reformed Church A Free Church formed in 1972 from a merger of the Congregational Church and the Presbyterian Church in England.

Vicar	One of the two designations of an incumbent of a parish. The other is 'rector'. Historically, the vicar stood in for a rector. (A team vicar or a team rector can also be designated vicar of a parish or a district even though neither is a vicar or a rector.)
Vox pop survey	Quick questions for an instant response: not scientific, more a snapshot of public opinion at one moment in time and place.
Word and sacrament	The two main aspects of a priest's liturgical role: preaching God's word and presiding at the sacraments of baptism and the Eucharist.
Word, service of the	A service of readings, prayers, hymns and sermon, but no Eucharist.
Workplace chaplain	A chaplain in places where people work. Workplace chaplains used to be called 'industrial chaplains' when there was more industry.
Youth for Christ	A voluntary organization that evangelizes among young people.
Youth worker	Someone who runs activities for young people or simply gets to know them and listens to them.